The Story of Ranch Hope

Dave Bailey

with Leo H. Carney

Gazelle
PRESS

ISBN 1-58169-151-3
For Worldwide Distribution
Printed in the U.S.A.

Gazelle Press
P.O. Box 191540 • Mobile, AL 36619
800-367-8203

Table of Contents

Dedication

This book is dedicated to my wife Eileen (co-founder of the Ranch), our daughter in heaven, Lee Ann, Elizabeth, and David, Jr. Without their love and support, there would be no ministry.

Preface

Ranch Hope for Boys and Girls was founded more than 40 years ago to bring hope to troubled youth. I have known Dave Bailey and have helped support his ministry for nearly two-thirds of that time. In my experience with raising my own children and the extended Williams family, I have seen the importance of both love and discipline. I have also realized that many young people need a second, even third chance, such as that which is available at Ranch Hope. In a family atmosphere, the Ranch Hope staff attempts to educate, counsel, train, and guide youth into an entirely new life in Jesus Christ.

We endorse this Christian ministry and hope that as you read this book you will be blessed by the miracle story of God building buildings and rebuilding troubled boys and girls.

—*Pat Williams*
Orlando Magic NBA Basketball Team

Foreword

When Mother Theresa was asked how she intended to feed a billion hungry children, her answer was, "One by one!" The same can be said about the great urban crisis that faces America. There is no special government program that is going to make things right. The only way urban young people are going to be rescued from the dismal prospects of their future is one by one. And that is what Ranch Hope is all about.

In the last 20 years, teenage crime has increased 10,000 percent. Juvenile courts have become overtaxed institutions because most of the major crimes in this country are now being committed by young people. Consider the fact that in some of the communities in which I am personally involved in ministry, more than 60% of males between the ages of 13 and 30 have already been convicted of a felony. Please note, these are not misdemeanors. I'm talking about rape, murder, armed robbery, etc. Also note that this figure only includes those who have been caught, tried, and found guilty. In the city of Philadelphia where I work and serve, the district attorney's office will readily admit that more than 10,000 convicted teenagers are free to roam the streets of the city for no other reason than there is no place to put them. All jail cells are filled. The prisons are obscenely overcrowded, and detention centers for juveniles are just about non-existent.

It was in response to circumstances such as I have been describing that Dave Bailey founded Ranch Hope.

Camden, New Jersey is just across the Delaware River from Philadelphia, and the conditions there may be worse than they are in Philadelphia. But it is not just Camden, and it is not just Philadelphia. It is also in smaller communities like Glassboro and Bridgeton that the problem of juvenile crime rears its ugly head. From all those places and more, Dave Bailey has taken in teenagers and endeavored to give them a whole new way of life through Jesus Christ.

One of the most prominent African-American sociologists on the contemporary scene is Julius Wilson. He points out that a major problem in black ghetto areas has been brought on by what most people would consider to be a blessing—I am referring to the end of legally sanctioned discrimination. In former times, when there was no escape for upwardly mobile African-American professionals, they were forced to live in the ghetto. There they provided role models for young men and women in the community. It was the African-American doctors, lawyers, college professors, teachers, and business executives that provided the cement that held those ghetto communities together.

With the end of discrimination, however, these people left the ghettos and moved to nicer neighborhoods. But they left behind a group of young people that is devoid of leadership models. Who is going to lead these people into a better way of life? Many of the young people who live in these urban asphalt jungles do not know a single adult male of their own race who has ever succeeded in anything or held down a permanent job.

Most of these young people believe they stand no chance of ever escaping from their dismal circumstances—and they are probably right.

Dave Bailey is a major part of what I call "God's Ambulance Squad." He and the members of his team are the ones who rush in and pick up casualties from this horrendous social system. Ranch Hope stands out as a divine instrument for rehabilitating those who have been severely wounded by the socio-economic injustices of this contemptible system.

But even as they pick up the casualties of the system, they know that for every one rescued, ten more are coming along to take his/her place. Sooner or later, the rest of us will have to face the question as to how to change the system itself. It's not enough that the heroic people of Ranch Hope are there to pick up those who are brutalized by the system. All of us together must ask, "How can we recreate the social system so that it doesn't do these sorts of things to young men and women?"

It should be further recognized that in most areas suffering from urban blight, the church is the only institution that can be an effective instrument for facilitating social change because it is the only institution that is left there. Businesses have fled. Schools have fallen into disrepair. Community organizations have evaporated. Only the church remains.

Those of us living in the suburbs must be ready to put people and money into these urban churches so that

they can do the job. Churches need to become incuba-
tors for small businesses. They have to do job placement. They have to do counseling. They have to
organize community people for rehabilitating buildings
and keeping the streets safe. They must become primary
agents for fighting against drug trafficking. It can be
done, and it must be done—but until it is done, there
will be Dave Bailey and Ranch Hope picking up the casualties, loving them in the name of Christ, and trying to
restore them to the life that God intended them to have.

—*Tony Campolo*
Professor Emeritus of Sociology
Eastern University
St. Davids, Pennsylvania

Aerial view of Ranch Hope

Chapter 1

Bailey, You Ought to Go Back to the Pulpit

I t took a long time and plenty of begging, borrowing, and persuading before what is now Ranch Hope began to resemble the dream God had put in my heart for helping troubled boys and girls.

We had the property and the 135 acres of abandoned farmland had been cleared before the first young people had ever arrived, but during the two years that followed the opening of Ranch Hope, my mind was still cluttered with the debris of doubt. The reality of Ranch Hope did not look like the dream—it wasn't working, and my resolve to proceed with what I thought was God's plan was shaky at best. There were a lot of questions and not nearly enough answers. Had I been wrong in the first place? Was I mistaken about the Lord's call on my life? *After all, Lord, wasn't it Your idea to create a residen-*

tial program for troubled boys and girls—the worst of the lot, the hardest cases, the ones who had nowhere else to go but the reformatory or death on the streets? Hello, Lord, are You there?

Maybe the idea of a western-style ranch in the East (in "New Joisey") wasn't as unusual or appealing as I had imagined. *Was it really Your vision, God, or was it just a fancy dance that Messiah Dave was doing in his own head?* Maybe I had watched Mickey Rooney and Spencer Tracey once too often in the movie *Boys Town*. Was my dream just a Father Flanagan delusion?

Should I go back to preaching from the pulpit? So much failure, so much criticism was coming my way. The boys and girls were getting worse here instead of better. *Who was that supposed to bless, Lord?*

People appreciated me more as a full-time preacher and youth pastor when I kept Jesus in church where He belonged—on Sundays, 10-11 A.M., and at youth meetings on Sunday evenings. Life certainly was simpler when I was working with middle class kids already in church, even if only due to parental mandate. A preacher could get by with ear-tickling Bible verses, a few "thee's" and "thou's," and some "shoulda-ought-coulda-mighta's." Sometimes, however, these church kids had needs as great as the so-called troubled ones. As disinterested churchgoers, unfortunately many were immune to the real Gospel. They were what I called "Churchians" rather than Christians.

Anyway, as long as it's confined to church, people sure do like Your stuff, Lord. They love to be hearers of the Word. I found out in 1964, Ranch Hope's first year, that as I tried to be a doer of the Word—to take Jesus beyond the walls of the temple and help feed His lost sheep—that some folks got plain nasty.

The Trial in Salem

Frank, one of the boys from the ranch had run away again. He had stolen a car, and the judge had sentenced him to Bordentown Reformatory (now Albert C. Wagner Youth Correction Facility) for four years. After the trial, the judge, with his stern demeanor and long black robes along with the detective, who was built like a linebacker, cornered me in a shabby, dimly lit back room of the Salem County Courthouse. The fearsome detective glared at me. "You're trying to jam Jesus down these kids' throats," he said. "It's not what they need. This Jesus stuff won't work!"

The judge agreed. Jail, they both maintained, was the only answer for troubled teens. "Bailey," the detective advised, "you ought to go back to the pulpit and leave kids like this to us."

They were telling me that Frank and others like him were unsalvageable—kids who were always going to be in and out of reformatories and prisons. Well, Frank eventually proved the detective wrong after being released from Bordentown. He now has a wife, three children, and a good job with a car manufacturer. And most importantly, he's never been incarcerated since. Nevertheless, to me, a 27-year-old preacher who wanted to show the world that Jesus Christ was alive and willing to help and heal the worst juvenile delinquents, these words from the judge and detective were fiery darts that deeply wounded my spirit.

The detective and the judge did have a point, though, or so it seemed at the time. After all, weren't the boys and girls who were sent to a Christian home for troubled youth supposed to *stay there* and be good. Why did *my* boys always run away and get arrested? Didn't they know that *my* reputation was to be valued more than great riches? Or was this really Ranch Hopeless that I was running? *Hello, this is serious Lord!*

In the early days, I was struggling with rehabilitating the boys as well as expanding the campus of the Ranch to accommodate more of them. We ran into unbelievable problems with construction—tradesmen who were incompetent, one was an alcoholic. Other workmen promised the world and then didn't even show up. My board of managers was beginning to question the direction in which we were headed. Our finances were dwindling, and we had an $18,000 mortgage, which in those days was big money. I began to wonder if God was throwing me a curve ball.

Well, looking back it doesn't take much for me to see that God was not throwing me a curve at all. The doubts I was struggling with were born out of my own immature walk with God. Only later did I learn that pain is often the admission price we must pay to experience the power and glory of a working relationship with our heavenly Father. Of all the fallacies and unreal expectations that people develop during childhood, perhaps the worst is that life is not supposed to be difficult. The early days of the Ranch were a time of great trial and testing for me. The Lord needed to take me through it so that I would be prepared for the bigger job ahead and also learn to trust in Him with all things.

As we trusted Him and moved ahead, God proved to be faithful. Today Ranch Hope is what He has made it by using us. It is the main residential treatment center for all state agency referrals of troubled boys and girls throughout most of southern New Jersey, in addition to private referrals, some of which come from outside the state. Keeping our eyes on the Lord, we have been able to build a ministry based on the principle found in Romans 15:1—"We then that are strong ought to bear the infirmities of the weak and not to please ourselves."

As our ministry progressed, we also saw ourselves as living the parables of Luke 16. I will illustrate those parables in more detail toward the end of this book, but basically we found ourselves in the business of searching for lost sheep—lost because of their own carelessness— and bringing them back into the fold. We also found ourselves searching for lost coins—lost because of someone else's carelessness or abuse. The woman in the parable searched her home relentlessly until she found her lost coin. She did not give up, even though she had other coins.

Luke 16 also tells the story of the prodigal son, who left home and family to wallow in the ways of the world. All his dad could do was wait and pray that his son would one day return. Eventually the rebellious boy did come home, but only after discovering that a life separate from his father was painful and not worth living. The prodigal's father rejoiced when the repentant boy returned. In one way or another, each of our young people is lost; each is somehow separated from God when we receive them and needs to be reunited. During the last quarter of a century, we at the Ranch have had many opportunities to rejoice with the heavenly Father when His boys are found and reunited with Him.

As it turned out, the only thing throwing me a curve was my own spiritual immaturity. Perhaps I expected things to go too smoothly just because I was doing God's will. Well, as I continue this wondrous story in the following pages, you'll see how smoothly things were not going.

Chapter 2

Dirtier by the Dozen

The incident at the courthouse and the construction and money problems were not our only trials. In these early days, potential discouragement came about once a week by the truckload. How, for example, could anyone working with tough kids, who had repeatedly been in trouble with th law, be naive enough to put them all to bed at night, alone and unwatched, and expect them to stay there? Keep in mind, our first dozen kids had arrived in fairly rapid succession.

It was easy for me to believe that they were staying in bed at night and behaving themselves since they were usually there for breakfast in the morning. I say "usually' because one glorious summer day when I went in to wake them, you guessed it, they were gone! Not one or two of them had disappeared—all 12 of them. My cries of "rise and shine" were met with a hollow silence.

There I was, left standing alone in the hallway of the small ranch house. I felt stupid. Here I was trying to transform the quality of these teens' lives. I had figured that all I needed to do was take them out of their terrible environment, give them a good place to live, feed them, and let Christ do the rest.

Although I had enjoyed some success with middle class kids while in the pastorate, this situation was altogether different. For one thing, my wife Eileen and I were the entire staff in those early days. Between the two of us we were houseparents, teacher, psychologist, medic, athletic instructor, cook, maid, and maintenance crew. Eileen was cooking every day for 16 people. She was also doing most of the washing and ironing. On top of that, our oldest child, Lee Ann, had birth defects and required special care, while our youngest, Liz, was still in diapers. There were few days off and no vacations at all.

I was still pastoring on Sundays at my local church near the Ranch. We didn't have our own chapel yet, so every Sunday morning we packed up the family and all the young people in a couple cars and herded them to the church service. You can imagine the scene. The young people's level of discomfort in church was beyond what you would describe as fidgety. It was hard to blame them for lack of control, however, for their entire lives were largely out of control. Anyway, Eileen and I soon learned that stress was the price to pay for not observing the biblical principle of Sabbath rest. Life can get a little too crazy without a day off in the Lord.

The Great Escape

Eileen and I were utterly collapsing around 11:00 P.M every evening. We were living in a small apartment at the end of Ranch Hope's first residence, Cowan Cottage. The kids, we assumed, were bedding down for the night at the other end of the cottage. Wrong!

These 12 kids had taken my blood, sweat, and tears and hit the trail. Gosh, was it something I had said? But this was no time for humor. The fact is, I was shocked the morning I found that they had all vanished. They didn't even leave a note or anything. Where do a dozen troubled teens go during the night in Salem County, New Jersey, five miles from the nearest anything? Yet, I had to admit the Great Escape had taken place. By the time I walked back to our apartment to commiserate with Eileen, my despair had turned to anger. Eileen broke down in tears. "Oh Dave, where did we go wrong?"

"Where did *we* go wrong..." I bellowed back at her, almost forgetting about the be-angry-but-do-not-sin rule. I was fuming. My thoughts turned from simply reporting the escape to county probation and never letting the boys return, to being filled with righteous indignation and determination. The Holy Spirit was rising up within me and reminding me exactly what my relationship was with them. They were family. They were my children. they had defied their "father," and now their "father" was going to find them and drag them home.

It took a couple days, but I finally rounded up all

dozen of them in a frantic door-to-door search that covered 200 miles. I personally found eight of them at home in their old neighborhoods. The other four were sent back by their parents. *What's next, Lord? Will you now reward Dave for his faithfulness and determination? Is this the part where I get blessed big time, Lord?*

A Ranch Hope Theft Ring

The Great Escape eventually revealed that most of the boys were regularly leaving at night after Eileen and I had gone to sleep. They would go home or visit a girlfriend or something. It was a bizarre revelation. To them, Ranch Hope was little more than a nocturnal hotel or a work-release program. They put in their time during the day, didn't miss a meal, and then, whenever they wanted, checked out for the evening.

Gradually we were able to hire a part-time houseparent who also served as a teacher and cook, to relieve me and my wife from the grueling schedule. In the process of doing that, however, we were to have an even worse experience than the Great Escape. One day I was helping clean our barn, which was now inhabited not by the old farm's original pigs, goats, and fowl, but mostly by horses. When I moved some bales of hay, there lay a stash of stolen goods—cigarettes by the case, watches, and other sundry items.

It quickly dawned on me what the boys were really doing when they slipped away at night. After some further probing and sleuthing, I coaxed a confession from one boy. Surprisingly, he spilled everything and named his accomplices. Yes, he admitted they were operating an organized theft ring and regularly were ripping off the local general store as well as parked cars, all under the cover of night. They had even appointed lookouts.

I learned that the state police had investigated the thefts, especially at the store, which had been broken into and robbed four times in seven weeks. When I asked the owner of the store why investigators had not been directed to me and the Ranch for the obvious reasons, the owner laid this one on me: "Well, Dave, to tell you the truth, the state police felt sure it was the work of professional thieves."

Riding back from the store that day, it occurred to me that not only had Ranch Hope been failing in its treatment and rehabilitation, it was a breeding ground for real delinquency. I was merely the dean of a graduate school where those with bachelors degrees in criminality could obtain further instruction and practical field work toward their masters' degrees. Their tuition was all paid for, and room and board were included. "That's just great," I said to myself. What I had believed was a divine plan for the healing of these boys had been perverted into the very antithesis of all I had dreamed about and worked toward. I could have kicked myself over my naivete.

Guilty?

As it turned out, five boys were charged by the state police with larceny and breaking and entering. Three others were passive lookouts or accomplices. The remaining four, despite other difficulties, were not part of the theft ring. Each one of these original 12 was truly a story in themselves.

When they first arrived to fill the beds at the brand new Ranch Hope, our expectations were high. Eileen even made the light-hearted remark that this was really the only way to have children—get someone to send them to you when they are 13-16 years old—and there would be no diapers, early childhood doctor bills, and especially, no labor pains. Her humorous aside still rings in our ears after all this time. Ironically, there was much pain to endure with these 12, and more labor than we ever imagined.

The Lord never gives us a dream or a vision without also providing the means to accomplish it. But through years of hard work and training, I have discovered that much diligent effort may be necessary before we are equipped to live out the dream and make it work as He planned. In the process of becoming thus equipped, we may stumble and fall many times. Like Job, we may often wonder why our faithfulness is merely being rewarded by additional failure and still more trials.

In my case, it was not until several years after starting the Ranch that I realized it had not been wise to accept every one recommended to us. During those early days, in what I believed at the time to be a true Christian attitude, we accepted anyone the courts asked us to take. The first dozen were all boys, but there was no prescribed screening or intake protocol such as we have today, and because of our simplistic, fresh-air philosophy of what it took to help a troubled youth, failures abounded among the original 12 boys.

We erred in mixing the severely emotionally disturbed together with those who were socially maladjusted. There was no distinction between them as there is now. We also mixed these first two categories with those who had hardened and violent sociopathic-type personalities. Added to this mix were those mildly troubled boys we seemed to get almost by accident. On top of all these problems, we unknowingly took on those with addiction problems. (This was a time when alcohol use and drugs were still considered mostly an urban problem among older kids.) We simply didn't know any better.

A Boy Named Tommy

One of the things the Lord had to teach us in the beginning was that troubled kids do not always have any immediately distinguishable physical or behavioral characteristics. There is no prototype—they come in all shapes, sizes, and colors. Some are assertive and loud; others are quiet and reserved.

These first 12 boys did not come accompanied by the elaborate paperwork and individual case histories that they come with now. We were only given basic information about their offenses and family situations. In those days, juvenile delinquency was just emerging from being viewed strictly as a law enforcement and correctional problem to one with individual psychological, sociological, neurological, and spiritual aspects. We were just beginning to understand troubled children in a more compassionate and systematic way, and as a consequence, discovering how to better help them. One thing we have learned since those days is that a kid who gets into trouble from time time is not necessarily what we call "troubled." A troubled child is one who is constantly in trouble at home, in school, in the streets, often with the cops and the courts getting involved. We consider ourselves blessed when we receive a youngster whose problem has been identified and acted upon early. More common at the Ranch, however, is the boy who has spent most of his early years in a brutal environment: physically and/or emotionally abandoned, raised by a single parent or perhaps a parent with an alcohol or drug problem, and abused sexually, emotionally, or physically. All this, of course, is lived out against the backdrop of a godless home.

Tommy was one of these. He was a kid who had us all fooled. Although his story is a tragic one, I thank God for Tommy and all that he and others like him have taught us. Tommy was a short, stocky boy of 13, red-haired and freckle-faced with a winning smile. He was an all-American, Rockwellesque-looking kind of boy whose image on a poster could raise a million dollars. He loved sports, and did we have fun together playing baseball and basketball! He was a good athlete. Tommy could not adjust to the lifestyle at the Ranch, however. He kept running away, mostly from reality and from himself.

On many occasions while checking up on the boys at night, I would enter his room and find Tommy sniffing cheap glue from a small, brown paper candy bag. He would do just about anything to get high, including placing his own sock over his face to sniff the noxious glue. I began to notice the effect this was having on his personality as he became less social, more withdrawn, and more dull-humored and angry. The last time Tommy ran away, he got in trouble and wound up at the Gloucester County courthouse in Woodbury, New Jersey. While awaiting his trial, he tried to commit suicide by sticking a wet finger in a light socket over the toilet. It didn't work, but the jolt sent him flying.

I once saw Tommy take glass from a broken light bulb and try to slit his wrists with it. On another occasion, upon being sentenced to do time in a correctional facility, he jumped through a glass window on the second floor of the courthouse and ran, cut and bleeding into a nearby Catholic Church, where he unsuccessfully tried to secret himself away. He was always caught, but he always kept on running. Tommy never stopped long enough for anyone to help him work through his problems. Some kids are just too hurt and scared and rebellious to give anyone a chance.

The Turnpike Murder

One night, a few years after Tommy had left us, I got a phone call, which was one of the most unintentionally cruel surprises I ever received. It was Tommy's mother.

"Reverend Bailey, Tommy has finally stopped running," she said.

"Praise God," I replied, "Did Tommy really accept Jesus this time and settle down to get his life together?"

"No," his mother replied, "they found his body along the Pennsylvania turnpike. He was shot and killed."

After further conversation and investigation, I learned that Tommy had been part of a team of hit men who worked between Florida and New York, committing contract murders. They would take turns on each hit. It was Tommy's turn to murder someone in Pittsburgh. That night, Tommy had tried to back out—I suspect I know why—and they shot him in the back of the head and once in the back. His body was then pushed out of the car alongside the Pennsylvania Turnpike. I learned that after he had left Ranch Hope at the age of 16, Tommy had become a big city drug dealer.

I gave the eulogy at Tommy's funeral, and the memories of our counseling sessions as well as the ballgames and other activities we shared haunted me and touched my heart with sadness. I had pictures on my office wall of young Tommy playing Ping-Pong with me.

Tommy's mother showed me a letter at the funeral that helped me stop blaming myself for what had befallen Tommy. "Mom," the letter read in part, "they're out to get me. The pigs won't leave me alone."

I also recalled that while Tommy was in school and at Ranch Hope, it was always the teachers who were out to get him or the cops who were against him. In fact, he felt that the whole world was against him, and nothing was ever his fault. Well, the pigs didn't get him; it was his buddies, the boys he ran with, who finally took his life. I try to get this important message across to the youth who come here—you can't keep running forever. Yes, even Tommy finally stopped running.

Truckin' for Jesus

Before concluding the theft ring story, I want to inject another highway tale, this one having a happy ending. God is in the business of producing happy endings for those who love and obey Him, and Bob Johnson's turned out to be one of them. Bob came to us when he was a skinny little blond guy whose family life and schooling was a nightmare.

For the first time in his life, he was eating and sleeping well, and being loved and cared for. He grew in Jesus and grew in stature, becoming a towering addition to our tag football and basketball teams at the Ranch. In fact, although a little older, he became good friends with my son Dave. Because of this friendship, he was a regular visitor to our home. The Bailey family became pretty close to this boy, who became transformed from a retiring little runt to an assertive personality with athletic prowess.

Bob graduated from the program here, lived on campus at Hope Home for a few years, and attended Christian camps during the summers. After graduating from high school, he contacted us to ask if the tuition help we provided for certain boys was limited to college, or if it included trucking school too. Bob saw himself as a trucker and wanted to receive the training needed to do it. We helped him with that training course and then with an advanced program that promised to place him in a job.

We began to suspect that something was up, however, when we didn't hear from Bob for quite a while after he left the last school. We prayed fervently that our worst fears would not be realized. Well, one evening a state trooper came to our door and asked me if I knew whose huge 18-wheeler was parked a few houses down the road. I told him I didn't, but later put two and two together when Bob, now a burly specimen of a man, showed up at the door. What a joy it was to see him and to learn that he was dating a girl he was serious about marrying! He had stopped by on his way to Maryland to look for a home for them. Well, years later, Bob stopped by again, this time bringing his lovely wife and two great children.

Having maintained his Christian walk and being

blessed by God, Bob is now trucking for Jesus up and down America's highways, an example of the good that God can do at a place called Hope.

You Made It Too Easy, Rev!

Returning to the theft ring story, the members of the Ranch Hope theft ring were charged by the state police and later appeared before a judge who sentenced them to the state reformatory at Jamesburg. It was a very emotional experience for all of us. My wife and I had become very close to two of the boys. I experienced all the feelings of sadness, remorse, humiliation, and love that any dad would feel if his kids were carted off to reform school.

In the heat of all this emotion, when the boys were being led out of the courtroom, one of the boys named John looked at me tearfully and said, "Rev, you made it too easy for us." I wanted to hug him and punch him out at the same time. His remark really hit home, though, and for quite some time I played it over and over in my head, searching for an answer. Had I made it too easy for this boy to remain stuck in his old ways? What did he mean, too easy? Was I too weak as an authority figure? Or was I expecting too little from myself and too much from the Lord in the healing of these boys? Perhaps my approach had been too simplistic and my faith not tempered enough by wisdom.

Chapter 3

God's Solution or Dave's?

In the process of searching for answers, I regularly sorted through my own childhood. One thing I knew for sure was that I had no problem identifying with these boys. Although my boyhood was not as conspicuously troublesome as theirs, I did grow up in a tough environment under difficult circumstances. I was the youngest member of the Bailey family, having five older siblings: Doris, Sarah, Clarence Jr., Frank, and Pip. We were very close growing up, but my father, Clarence Salathiel Bailey, was the child of an alcoholic father with whom he had a very poor relationship.

Dad was raised on a farm in Virginia and was a hard man. I escaped the severe discipline that my brothers regularly received because I was younger by eight years. I recall looking on in horror when I was four as my father struck them repeatedly. I resolved to be so good

that a similar fate would not befall me. Even though he had become anti-alcohol and rarely touched a drink, Dad could still be abusive. H was a loving father but an angry man, who from time to time would lose control and lash out violently at his kids. Thankfully he never laid a finger on my mother, Stella, who was a good wife and a strong maternal figure. Dad had a typical Jekyll and Hyde personality, though he did grow more mellow as he aged.

My Boyhood Revisited

We lived in a ramshackle house in Penns Grove, New Jersey, on a farm-like piece of property in a nice residential neighborhood. My dad was a good provider and a hard-working man, laboring at the nearby E.I. DuPont DeNemours Company. He supplemented his salary by having the family raise, prepare, and sell chickens, eggs, turkeys, and farm produce. I learned the meaning of hard work. Oddly enough, I think I developed my desire to work with kids from my father. He was the first man in Salem County to start a Boy Scout Troop. This was a clear indication to me that, although Dad seldom went to church, the Lord somehow had managed to reign in a corner of his heart. My familiarity with farming and animals later made the the idea of establishing a ranch for youth—complete with all the critters—seem very natural indeed. The Bailey family used to proudly "put out" 1000 oven-ready turkeys and chickens at Thanksgiving and Christmas. I was slaughtering, boiling, plucking, and delivering birds as far back as I can remember. We used to hang them up on the outhouse in the backyard.

When I was seven, my brothers and sisters were old enough to go off to World War II or to work in defense plants. After they left, I was brought up as sort of an only child. I had two brothers in the Army, one in the Navy, and a sister was an Army nurse. Four stars hung in our window at home. They were my early heroes. But when the war ended, they came home for a short time, married, left home, and I was again the only Bailey left with Mom and Dad at home.

I had a nimble and sarcastic tongue and a penchant for comic entertainment. These virtues enabled me to become the class clown. It seemed like fun, and I got a lot of attention as I was thrown out of school or pounded by one of the targets of my practical jokes or wisecracks. I was totally rebellious in school from the seventh grade on, although I wouldn't have dared to pull my funny stuff at home. I was a bit of a Jekyll and Hyde. In addition to being a big-time brat, because of my mother's influence, I attended the Methodist Church each Sunday and sang in the choir. I sang one tune on Sundays and a different one the rest of the week.

I still get embarrassed when I run into a former teacher or fellow student who kids me about my dramatic protest against girls wearing jeans to school, which was an abomination in the late 1940s. I registered my protest by coming to school one day wearing a dress. The principal, not thinking that I was cute, suspended me. My prank even made the headlines of the local newspaper. However, my attitude toward the authority of my parents was also miserable. For example, my stealing Dad's truck for joy riding was a common occurrence all the while he was working hard to support our family.

That Saving Grace

David Lee Bailey was such a source of trouble and frustration to his teachers that one of them told me privately in the balcony of the school auditorium that if she had her druthers, she would throw me off the balcony right then and there. She had grabbed me by the hair on the back of my head and told me that the only thing preventing her from hurling me over the edge was the possibility of a jail sentence. That scared me. Once again, though, the class clown resumed pushing the envelope to the edge.

A turning point came in my turbulent school career when I began to listen to Tom Robinson, a teacher who talked to me whenever I was being punished in the principal's office—which was often. He was a special person who told me I had great untapped potential and that a wonderful future awaited me. He told me that if I could just convert the energy that I was using to be a jerk into positive behavior, I could make something more of myself than a fool.

Mr. Robinson stayed with me and never gave up. I tell my staff today that they must stick with young people for a long time and never give up on anyone. The Bible says the Lord rewards a man who perseveres. It paid off in my case with Mr. Robinson. In my sophomore year of high school, I took my popularity as the class clown and traded it in for a seat on the student council. Mr. Robinson and I had found a formula for success. Although my grades did not improve for quite a while, my attitude did. So, in addition to proving the old political adage that people often put clowns into office, my experience also demonstrated to me that troubled children can respond marvelously to love acceptance, and caring. There is an old hymn that says, "Oh, how I love Jesus...because He first loved me." The Word of God similarly tells us that while we were still in sin and unsaved, God loved us and sent His only Son, Jesus Christ, to forgive our sins and offer us a place with Him in eternity. So it is that the first step in the healing of troubled young people is that they need to be shown the love of God and told of their potential for good by adults who won't give up on them. From a strictly human and secularly viewpoint, this is not an easy thing to do. From a Christian point of view, it is the *only* thing to do.

At about the same time my path was beginning to straighten out in school, my father had a heart attack and shortly thereafter, a stroke. His employer placed him on full disability, which put the family in a bad financial situation. We had just moved from a run-down house to a new one in a new neighborhood. For the first time in my life, at the age of 15, we had an indoor toilet and a real bathtub to replace the galvanized one we had known for so many years. I guess you could say it was like moving from the outhouse to the penthouse.

At that time my folks were also raising my niece, Beverly, because of some difficulties my sister Sarah was having. Dad did what he could to make money, and I delivered newspapers and sold eggs after school to help the family save some money for college, a prospect that was not looking very good despite all my hard work. I blew some of that money on a '35 Plymouth coupe which my parents never knew about until it ended up in the junkyard, and I was broke. April of my senior year I found a small Quaker college in North Carolina called Guilford College, which had a relatively modest tuition. My chances of getting there were slim. Even though I had a few hundred dollars saved for living expenses, the tuition was still $750.

Despite his poor health, my father took to the streets during the long, hot summer following my high school graduation. While I was considering joining the armed forces instead of going to college, he was doggedly selling newspaper subscriptions. I recall him coming home at the end of the day, totally exhausted and soaked with sweat. Before the end of the summer, though, Dad had sold a record number of subscriptions. But it was what he did next that really blew me away. He gave me almost all the money I needed for my first year of college. Clarence Bailey, a hard-working laborer with an eighth grade education, wanted more than anything to see his youngest son go to college. This once turbulent man was capable of great sacrifice.

The Ministry

I went away to Guilford College, fully intent on eventually studying law. My uncle, Judge Alvin Featherer, was a prominent attorney and promised me I could take over his successful practice one day if I became a lawyer. He even said he would pay for law school. This gave my father and me a great incentive, but I soon blew the family dream. During my freshman year at college I attended a Billy Graham rally in Greensboro, North Carolina. I went forward and accepted the Lord and a short time later began hearing the Lord's call to the ministry. My law career was going down the tubes fast, much to the disappointment of my father and uncle. The two most important men in my life were very unhappy with me over my final decision to study for the ministry, each thinking, "Where have I gone wrong?" It was a painful paradox—feeling love, accepted, and honored by God, but rebuked and rejected by key members of my family. My mother, on the other hand, was happy for me. She was supportive, although somewhat ambivalent about my choice.

About six months after I had accepted the Lord at the Billy Graham rally, I transferred to Western Maryland College near Baltimore and began seriously considering the ministry. One Sunday evening something happened in my dormitory room that showed what a long way I still had to go in my spiritual walk. I learned that although I had one foot in God's Kingdom, I also had one foot in the world. A bunch of guys and I were fooling around, telling off-color jokes and stories about the campus coeds. A good friend, George Douglas, walked into the room as all this was going on and listened to me for a while.

George asked if I had been to church that morning. "Yes," I replied, "Why?" George was 27 then, and I was only 20 years old. I admired him greatly as a fellow athlete and mentor, so what he said next had a great impact on me.

"Dave," he said, "I thought you were a Christian. You were in church this morning, and you're talking like this tonight? You're not my kind of Christian." With that, he walked out of the room. He was a good witness to have the guts to talk to me like that. His admonition humbled me greatly, and in fact, marked the beginning of my spiritual metamorphosis. George later helped me come to grips with my spirituality and my commitment. Those few simple but strong words spoken by a fellow Christian, whom I admired, convicted me of the Lord's desire for me to reevaluate my personal lifestyle. It was all there in His Word, the Bible, and I'll always be grateful to George for helping me see it.

The New Bailey and Family

In my senior year at Western Maryland College, I married my high school sweetheart from Penns Grove High School, Eileen Brown, who came to Maryland and worked as a telephone operator, allowing me to complete my senior year. Throughout the years, she is the person through whom God has blessed me the most.

After graduation in 1957, our life together seemed to move ahead full speed. I pastored my first church as a weekend commuter with Eileen by my side. At this time I was working for my bachelors of divinity degree at Temple University. When the school closed in my senior year, I enrolled at Martin Luther King Jr.'s alma mater, Crozer Seminary in Chester, Pennsylvania (now Colgate Rochester Divinity School). Each weekend we would drive home to Salem County to conduct services at Aldine Methodist Church. As the Lord would have it, Aldine was where I first met Hiram Strang, one of Ranch Hope's earliest benefactors. I also came to know his wife Florence and several other fine folks in that congregation, some of whom eventually became members of the Ranch's board of managers. I began an extensive youth ministry at Aldine.

Never one to let an opportunity to creatively spread the Gospel pass me by, I started *The Wondrous Story* radio broadcast in nearby Bridgeton over WSNJ, the oldest FM radio station in New Jersey. It was a daily devotional format with news and music. This was in 1958, and at that time I had no way of knowing that all these pursuits—the radio ministry, helping kids part time, and meeting concerned people—in a few short years would be mightily used by God just a few miles down the road from Aldine in Alloway, New Jersey. One of my most marvelous experiences has come from living long enough and close enough to God to be able to look back and see how His plan has unfolded. Eileen and I have been blessed this way.

We would never have imagined, however, that part of that plan included our beloved first child, Lee Ann, who was born severely handicapped in 1959. She was hydrocephalic, had *spina bifida* (a severe spinal defect), and had club feet. Through Lee Ann, the Lord showed us the reality of His tireless love and devotion and precisely how much strength He could bless us with when Eileen and I felt we were on the verge of physical and emotional collapse, which was almost daily. Lee died at the Ranch 11 years later. At first her disability was a Job-like experience for Eileen and me, what with all our other responsibilities, the endless doctor bills with the resultant terrible indebtedness. In the end, however, we passed the test of faith, and Lee Ann's life implanted in our hearts a burden for impaired children of all kinds. The Lord further blessed us with two additional children, Elizabeth and David Jr., who are healthy and love the Lord. Dave Jr. is now the Executive Director at the Ranch, and Liz is a teacher in public school. They have blessed us with five grandchildren.

While it is true that the family I came from had its

problems, God has given me a heart for holding onto the positive experiences of my upbringing and home life, and eventually letting go of the negative memories—the things that create affliction in some people. Not that I walked away from my childhood totally unscathed—I don't mean to say that at all. I agree with the maxim that what life does to us can make us bitter or better. God has allowed me to have *better* rather than *bitter* results. My childhood showed me what I did not want to become. I didn't want to emulate some of my father's negative behavior but rather pick up his great work ethic and ability to relate so well to others. I also did not want to emulate the young adult lifestyles of many of my peers. I wanted Christ in my life. Perhaps the sensitivity and caring I developed for my own child within—the spiritual child of God—enabled me to relate to troubled children, the bottom-of-the-barrel kids, the way He wanted me to relate. The Lord let me choose to be the antithesis of my father in those important ways, and I hope I have been faithful to that choice and to Him.

My mother, brothers, and sisters have always encouraged me, with Pierson (Pip) often helping with construction. My Dad passed away just before we bought the farm, but I am convinced that he came to know the Lord before his death.

The Vision

When I was 22, I found myself in court one day

trying to help Chris, a 16-year-old boy to whom I was a "big brother" while serving as youth pastor at Pitman Methodist Church. Chris had been charged with breaking and entering. He seemed to be one of my early failures—repeatedly getting into trouble and finally winding up on probation under my recognizance. When Chris was returned before the judge for violating his parole, we lost the battle. The judge refused to give him any more probation and instead sent him to Jamesburg State Reformatory for an indefinite term.

As I left the courtroom, Chris' caseworker from school turned to me and said, "Reverend Bailey, isn't it a shame we don't have a place here in New Jersey to reach these kids before they are sent to the reformatory?" As she spoke those words, my mind and emotions became totally consumed with the idea that I somehow would be the one to create the place she was talking about. In that one fleeting moment, God planted a seed within me that began to germinate even as I walked down the steps leaving the courthouse. *Yes,* I thought to myself, *it is a genuine shame that there isn't a place for troubled youth to get help before they end up in a reformatory— or before they end up dead.* That was in 1960.

Some months before this, after giving a talk on juvenile delinquency to local businessmen, a man came up to me in the banquet room. "Reverend Bailey," he said, "that was an interesting talk, but all the way through it I couldn't help wondering something. So now I'll ask you. What are you doing about it?" I was dumfounded. At that moment I had no answer for him. However, walking down the courthouse steps that day, I knew that God was answering the man's question in His way. Dave Bailey was going to establish a home for troubled youth somewhere, somehow, because the Lord had saturated every fiber of my being with that very specific vision. I couldn't have ignored it even if I had tried my hardest. My path had been established.

Lord, Did You Change Your Mind?

Although I was immediately consumed with the idea of establishing a place for troubled youth, I was painfully aware that, while the Lord had instilled the vision within me, at this point it was only a fuzzy black-and-white photograph. It did not come to me complete with an architectural drawing of a site plan, fund-raising instructions, or a three-year business plan—all of which I needed. And with so much going on in my life as it was—I was still pastoring two local churches, doing youth evangelism, and working the radio ministry— God's timing did not seem right to me. There was a lot of legwork He wanted me to do. And I probably would have been terribly disillusioned had I known in 1960 as I attempted the above things that it would be another four years before the doors of the Ranch would finally open.

I suppose it was my blessed ignorance and the grace of the Almighty that pushed me onward. Something else that propelled me forward was Ranch Hope's first angel in the person of Hiram Strang. Mr. Strang was a hard-working dairy farmer and member of my church at Aldine. I visited his home one evening to tell him that my nine month search for a piece of land had produced an abandoned 95-acre farm with a farmhouse, outbuildings, and barn in Alloway. I needed $10,000, which was the difference between the sales price and the existing mortgage. My plan, as I outlined it to him and his wife Florence, was to obtain twenty $500 loans. I asked Mr. Strang if he would be the first to make such a loan.

After what seemed like an eternity of deliberation, the rugged-looking dairyman stood up, cleared his throat, and said that he couldn't lend me $500. My heart sank. But it soared as he announced that he would lend the entire $10,000 at no interest with no schedule of payments. I rejoiced. The victory of Jesus Christ permeated me and my vision, and my wife and I praised the Lord all the way home that night. The 95 acres were ours!

By 1963, a bit more money had been raised, and the laborious and seemingly never-ending task of cleaning up the cluttered old farm was underway. The realization of Ranch Hope would have never come about without the dynamic group of women volunteers that came together that year—the Salem County Ranch Hope Auxiliary. These women provided our very first fundraising drive and much needed publicity, which included our annual rodeo in nearby Cowtown under the guidance of a men's group called the Wranglers. It also included an effort by one woman who bicycled door-to-door selling tiny concrete blocks that said, "Buy a block, Build a boy." They were great.

By the spring, Eileen, our two little daughters, and I moved into the dilapidated farmhouse where we would live a sort of rural ghetto-type existence until the first ranch house was completed a year later. That same year the board of managers was formed, composed of eight members drawn from a broad spectrum of the area's Christian community. Probation departments and school boards began officially recognizing Ranch Hope in 1964, the year the Dirty Dozen began to arrive.

As I have said, this period was not exactly my dream come true. The first couple of years were not the happily-ever-after I hoped for. Quite the opposite proved to be the case. We were so plagued by construction problems, incompetent labor, and a lack of money that I found myself contending with the Lord and half believing that somehow I had gotten the vision all wrong.

For instance, there was Arnold, a blustery, bearded, long-haired hulk of a man who roared onto the ranch in a souped-up 1947 Ford one day, mufflers blazing. At first he reminded me of the Apostle Peter, but as he jumped out of his car, he announced that he was the mason we had been searching for to finally construct our first building.

"Where's Reverend Bailey?" he shouted. "Where's Reverend Bailey? Praise God, I'm a mason, and the Lord sent me here to help you."

With that declaration, we praised God too. And we immediately appointed Arnold to be the head of construction. What a sorry decision that was! Arnold, God bless him, turned out to have only one good eye and a major drinking problem. We discovered he was spending extended lunch hours in the woods, downing beers with his helper. After he and I expressed fundamental disagreement over what constituted a straight line, Arnold was discharged from his messianic duties. We spent a lot of time and money correcting the crooked work he had done in laying block, if that's what you called it.

The lesson here is that if a biblical figure shows up praising the Lord and says he's on assignment for the Almighty, check his earthly credentials first.

It didn't get any easier with the next building. I recall early one evening walking down to the shambles that were the start of our second ranch house, Turrell Cottage. I felt like Nehemiah must have felt when he first surveyed the crumbled walls of Jerusalem. The shell of the building was up, but there were numerous cinder blocks just laying there. Concrete was left unpoured. The place was a wreck. There were no laborers to continue the work, and winter was soon to arrive. As I sat on one of the unfinished walls, I experienced Nehemiah's "sorrow of heart" when he addressed King Artaxerxes: "Why should not my countenance be sad, when the city lieth waste, and the gates thereof are consumed with fire" (Neh. 2:3).

Well, the gates of the ranch hadn't been actually

burned up, but like Nehemiah, I was "dreadfully afraid" that my dream was going up in smoke. The board of managers was similarly apprehensive and dutifully expressed this to me. There, alone in the "ruins" of Turrell Cottage, I began to pray that the Lord would send me some help, at least a sign, to encourage me in what I still wanted to believe was His vision. I spoke to God what Nehemiah has spoken to the king: "If it please the king, and if thy servant have found favour in thy sight, that thou wouldst send me unto Judah, unto the city of my fathers' sepulchres so that I may build it" (v. 5). I did not challenge God or try to cut a deal with Him; I never have. But in the fading twilight of that building that night, I put out a fleece, like Gideon, and asked for a definite sign that God wanted me to continue on with the dream.

Hello, Lord. It's Me Again!

I'll tell you later exactly how that symbolic fleece was touched by God. What I want to tell you now as this chapter closes is the burden that began to be lifted from my shoulders even as I walked back to the farmhouse that night. It's the power of prayer. For those of us who were not brought up as children in a trusting, reassuring, and dependable environment by godly parents, it is not always easy to hand over our will and our life to the Lord, even though we have come to Him and been born again in the spirit. The renewing of the mind and the healing of emotional scars can take longer, often lagging behind the renewal of the spirit. We have seen this often at Ranch Hope.

Nevertheless, I also want to tell you that there is great joy and confidence in giving up and surrendering our mountains of adversity to the Lord. When we truly cast our cares upon Him, knowing that He cares for us and will turn our sadness into joy, our burdens become more bearable. So I took courage that night after I had given over my problems to the Lord of my life. I knew I would eventually hear from Him. Although the flame within me was only flickering, I felt that somehow the vision was still alive and was not just a figment of my egocentric imagination. Nothing on this earth is *supposed* to be perfect except our desire for God, and that certainly applies to Ranch Hope and its mission.

Absalom and the Ranch

As I was recalling the terrible tragedy of Tommy's murder with some friends one time, I told them about King David and his rebellious son, Absalom. Absalom eventually became so destructive that he gathered together an army to conquer his own father's kingdom. He failed, however, and was killed in the battle by King David's own commander. Afterwards, lamenting his son's death, David cried, "Absalom, Absalom, my son Absalom, would God I would have died for you." It was too late, however. Absalom had embraced the darkness; he had first died spiritually, and now he was physically dead.

At Ranch Hope we have had parents, boys, probation officers, and caseworkers who have sat in our offices and said, "Would God, I could have died for this boy." Dave Bailey cannot give his life for the youth who come here. Not one of us can give us his or her life for one of the young people in our cottages today, but we can introduce them to the One who did.

I eagerly awaited the Lord's reply. My question had been how to help dead-end kids. Now I was asking Him if Ranch Hope was truly the answer.

Before we continue on with my story, in the next chapter let's look at how our nation came to experience the break-up of so much family life and what effect this had on the youth.

Chapter 4

A National Disgrace

I n the 1980s, our nation suffered briefly from the delusion that juvenile delinquency was waning. Not only did it turn out that the decrease was attributable to a decline in the population of 11-18 year olds, but by the mid-1980s, the figures began to rise again in several categories that measure the kinds of trouble that these kids get into. From 1988-1997, the total juvenile delinquency caseload rose 48%. As if that is not startling enough, in 1997 it was 400% of what it was in 1960![1]

About 1200 young people have passed through Ranch Hope in four decades. We are among 3,200 public and private facilities of all descriptions nationwide that provide custody and care for more than 100,000 children daily. These are kids who are wards of juvenile courts, juvenile corrections, or private agencies. The majority of juveniles in residential placement (72%)

were confined during afterschool hours by at least one locked door or gate.[2] Juvenile residential placement facilities vary in their degree of security. The use of fences, walls, and surveillance equipment is increasingly common in juvenile facilities, although security hardware in juvenile facilities is generally not as elaborate as that found in adult jails and prisons.

According to the federal government, the facilities provide a variety of residential programs for juveniles who are either accused or adjudicated delinquents, or what we call "status offenders"—runaways, incorrigibles, or truants. Some facilities are for kids detained or committed for treatment or placement as a result of abuse, dependency, neglect, or other reasons. These include juvenile detention centers, shelters, reception and diagnostic centers, training schools, group homes, as well as camps and ranches such as ours, which are predominantly in the western half of the nation and the south.

The U.S. Department of Justice tells a grim story of the price our nation is paying for raising children without love, in broken and ungodly homes, where the demons of divorce, adultery, alcoholism, drug abuse, and secular lifestyles run rampant.

Nearly all of these children (95%) were held for delinquent offenses, which are acts that would be considered crimes if they were committed by adults. The remaining 5% were held for status offenses or were detained or committed because they were abused, neglected, or dependent. According to the Office of Juvenile Justice and Delinquency Prevention, delinquency cases in 1997 totalled an appalling 1,755,100.[3] Of that number, 109,800 were listed as violent crimes, such as criminal homicide, forcible rape, robbery, and aggravated assault. There were 182,400 cases for drug law violations, and 595,300 cases were considered property crimes, such as burglary, larceny, motor vehicle theft, and arson.

Children in Custody

A trend of rising admissions and discharges was detected in 1989. In that year, the volume of juvenile admissions and discharges was the highest since 1970, totaling 1,228,000. That was the total number of times that the doors to places like correctional facilities and detention centers opened and closed. Most of the kids were held in public institutions. Blacks, Hispanics, and other minorities constituted 60% of the custodial population.

In 2001, those placed in residential detention, in the age group of 14 and under, totalled almost 17,000 kids or 16% of the total juveniles. The total number juveniles 18 and younger in detention was 104,413.[4] Drugs and alcohol continue to play a major role with juveniles. Although consumption of alcoholic beverages is illegal for those under 21 years of age, 10.4 million current drinkers were ages 12-20 in 1999. Of this group, 6.8 million engaged in binge drinking, including 2.1 million who would also be classified as heavy drinkers.[5]

These officially documented trends in juvenile delinquency are extremely important. They serve as a barometer of our social and spiritual climate as a nation. Troubled, hurting kids grow up, get married, and produce generation after generation of additional hurting kids. These figures also point out what, in my judgment, is a national disgrace and a terrible failure.

A Moral Failure

This increase in juvenile crime points to a severe moral failure in marriage and child rearing. As fathers and mothers, many Americans seem to be abdicating responsibility for rearing our children who are the lifeblood of the nation and our future. The increasing number of juveniles under confinement coupled with the decline in the juvenile population means that an ever-greater proportion of the juvenile population is being held in custody. The trend in the 1990s was, in part, one of giving up our children to the government because we have fallen short as both adults and parents.

Today, every 26 seconds someone under 18 runs away from home, and more than one million young people run away from home each year. Although 70% of runaways return home or are reunited with their families, 30% of them fall victim to violence, crime, prostitution, or starvation on the street.

The number of children being held for serious, violent offenses (murder, non-negligent manslaughter, robbery, and aggravated assault) began increasing in the late 1980s at a rate of 4% or more per year. The increase for females, who represent one in five of the juveniles in custody, was about 8%, double that of males. This appears to be further evidence of a loss of the traditional male and female roles in our society. The violence and anti-social behavior that was once taboo for girls and young women is now more common, even if it is present only in a small segment of the population.

While the emergence of this small percentile of the female juvenile population of the United States represents an extreme, the very appearance of the extreme can be seen as a barometer of the serious spiritual affliction among our female population as a whole. It tells us that this aggressive behavior among females is tolerated in the 21st century.

The Cost

The Bible admonishes us to "count the cost." The spiritual cost of childhood dysfunction translates into a financial curse as well—money that could be spent on cultural and spiritual upbringing is being robbed from our children and their families. The total annual operating costs of state and local governments administering juvenile facilities, which comprise over half of all such facilities in the nation, is $1.67 billion and rising. It costs anywhere from $17,600 to $78,800 per resident each year to keep a child in custody, according to Justice Department figures.

These figures do not begin to tell the economics of hurting kids, though. For instance, if you add together all the costs to local school boards of evaluating troubled boys and girls, the costs of things such as vandalism, medical bills, imprisonment in later years, and diminished overall lifetime earnings and productivity, we are more than likely looking at a total cost to our nation of many billions of dollars annually. That cost can be almost doubled when you count the other kids who are in private facilities like Ranch Hope.

And what about the kids who don't get caught or who slip through the cracks? What about kids who come from well-to-do families and receive private counseling for their delinquent behavior? It is likely that we're then talking about an overall loss to our nation that soars into the tens of billions of dollars. Think about that if you will. The cost of being unconcerned, irresponsible parents in the secular society of the new millennium will cost tens of billions of dollars. Astounding, isn't it?

Decade of Violence—Baby Boomerang

Individual states report their statistics on juvenile delinquency more frequently and effectively than does the federal government. Arrest figures alone, however, do not present a complete picture of the juvenile delinquency problem. For example, the New Jersey State Police Uniform Crime Report is the total number of crimes reported to the police and arrests made by the police. Many juvenile offenses don't lead to an arrest, and changes in arrest policies and practices by individual communities over time can create the illusion of either a declining arrest rate or a crime wave.

Nevertheless, it is interesting to note that a 1990 report in New Jersey declared a trend of decreasing juvenile delinquency through the decade of the 1980s—a decline of about 22%. It reported that the 1980s witnessed a clear decline in the number of juvenile arrests, even arrests for the more serious index offenses (murder, rape, robbery, aggravated assault, burglary, larceny theft, and motor vehicle theft). "This is certainly good news," the report said. It went on to attribute the decrease to the declining juvenile population. It then said, "We did, however, see an increase in arrests for violent index offenses in 1989, an abrupt turn around from the recent downward trend and a cause for concern."

That concern heightened as the report continued: "Demographers suggest that juvenile populations in the United States will soon be going up—reflecting something that has been termed the 'baby boomerang.' This, along with other recent trends, i.e., increased drug involvement and related violence," the report said, "portends trouble. Some have even predicted a decade of violence. Combined, these factors lead to markedly higher nationwide projections for delinquency, especially involving serious offenses."

The accuracy of this prestigious commission's prediction of 1990 was proved the very next year. Noting a 13.2% increase in violent index offense arrests for the year 1990, the 1991 report's language became more striking as it called the figure "particularly disturbing." "Combined with an expected increase in the general juvenile population in the 1990s and predictions that delinquency may increase in this population group, we can anticipate some rougher times ahead," the report predicted. Rougher times indeed. Murder, rape, robbery, and aggravated assaults among New Jersey's juveniles have soared 30.6% since 1988, the report states.[6]

A Serious Challenge

Whatever the variables or other interpretations of these state and federal statistics on troubled kids might be, we are not speaking here about a couple of percentage points one way or the other. Moreover, increases of 13% and 30% in recorded offenses statewide and the record rise in drug and alcohol offenses of 150% in only five years definitely sends up a red flag. Even as this book was being researched, the need to share what we know about the problems of dead-end kids was confirmed by the latest statistics. The problem is as bad as it has ever been in the history of our country.

What we've known all along in the spirit has now been indisputably supported by these secular statistics. Satan has struck a serious blow to the very fabric of our society—children and the family. We at Ranch Hope and other child care providers sound the alarm: Our society is being sabotaged by the enemy, and it's time to dress for battle. Stand strong and be of good courage. If we will fight, the victory will be ours

Commenting on the federal statistics, Robert V. Sweet. Jr.. administrator of the Office of Juvenile Justice arid Delinquency Prevention, had the following to say as the decade of the 1990s began: "Whether these increases are the result of greater involvement of our youth in delinquency or of more vigorous intervention by the police and juvenile courts, we cannot say with certainty. Whatever the reason, these numbers alone offer a warning. To have this many juveniles in public confinement every day of the year is too many. When doors of juvenile detention centers open 500,000 times a year to detain a troubled or dangerous youth, it is too many times."[7]

Of course, a decade later those figures are doubled. According to Mr. Sweet, these statistics represented a serious challenge that we see now has not been met. Parents must provide guidance and supervision, schools must teach the most hard-to-reach children, and our churches must become involved in helping parents rear their children to respect themselves and others.

It continues to be a challenge that needs our utmost attention. Farming and the family have never been the same since about the 1920s and '30s. Why farming? Well, agriculture required a family effort and family support system in order to thrive. Historically, farming provided an economic as well as spiritual and emotional bonds that generally kept families united under the same roof, in the same community, working together as a team.

Life was simpler, although perhaps not easier, in the 1930s. It certainly was not perfect and without sin. But Dad, after all, was generally the head of the family—the chief worker, provider, and protector. On or off the farm, Mom bore and nurtured the children, cooked, and kept the house. While Dad was the titular and spiritual head of the house, Mom was his all-important encourager and power source. This mutual reliance made for a God-given team, which despite its human flaws and failings, still pretty much functioned as He intended until around the 1920s and '30s.

The family was meant to be the basic human institution and building block of God's Church. But several important changes occurred back then in both the Church and family, which we'll discuss briefly. For one thing, there was severe drought in the mid-west, the nation's "breadbasket." It turned once rich farming soil into what they called the Dust Bowl. Then, there was the Great Depression—a near collapse of the national economy caused by several factors including the stock market crash of late 1929. The Dust Bowl and the Great Depression saw families deserting their farmland for the cities, pursuing other livelihoods or crumbling under the burden of sudden poverty. Because a much larger percentage of people lived on farms in those days than now, the economic impact was enormous.

Other factors affected the family at least as much as the Dust Bowl and Depression. The population of the nation began to swell and so did the size of our cities. The Depression saw President Franklin Delano Roosevelt initiate numerous public work projects. Among other things, these projects started what was to become our national highway system. It became easier to get from New York to Chicago, from Los Angeles to Seattle, or from Chicago to New Orleans.

America's love affair with the automobile picked up momentum. Cars and public transportation were cheap. The United States was becoming more transient, more mobile, and in the process, the neighborhood community became less stable, more dynamic. The nation began leaving behind the simple life and the security and rootedness of family. As the relatively unchanging and familiar communities that people were born and raised in began to disappear, church life and worship began to change, too. Families, it seemed, were not as accountable to a local church or synagogue as they used to be. Corporate America was ever changing and ever demanding. Families were suddenly uprooted and transferred from place to place every few years.

Of course, there are those who would argue that we never were a truly godly nation, that immorality, lawlessness, and domestic discord go back to our founding days. Why, these people might ask, are you pointing to the 1930s? Well, while it's true that such godlessness did exist long before the 1930s, ours was still a fundamen-

tally Christian culture back then. God and the
Scriptures had been at the very foundation of that culture since the American Revolution and the signing of
the Declaration of Independence.

When Things Got Worse

The decade of the 1920s had an effect on the 1930s
in terms of the family and morality. Both prohibition
and the prosperity following World War I had whetted
our baser appetites with images of shiny cars, provocative styles of clothing, and the secretive conclaves of immorality known as speak-easies. Immorality was going
public in the 1920s, yet even then the immorality was
confined to a minority that was largely condemned by
the more conservative majority. Most people were trying
to hold fast to the nation's Judeo-Christian ideals.

While proponents of secularism and humanism were
largely unknown as a group even in the 1920s, by 1933
an established organization known as the Humanist
Society issued its first Humanist Manifesto.[8] The godless
credo it espoused was essentially that man, as the center
of the universe, was a law unto himself. According to the
humanists of 1933 and today (a second Humanist
Manifesto was issued in 1973), there are no absolutes,
no right or wrong, no good or evil, except that which
man, not God, decides. Man is his own standard and the
ultimate measure of all things. This humanistic philosophy is the "gospel of self" and is mentioned in the Bible

(see 2 Tim. 3). It has pervaded our society since the 1930s and has become the cultural basis for today's growing immorality and lawlessness, which are antithetical to Christianity. The results of this philosophy has turned children against their parents, parents against their children, and young people against marriage and family. It results in the self becoming all important. But Jesus said we should deny ourselves, take up our cross, and follow Him.

Some of the socioeconomic changes of the 1930s—the beginning of our so-called modern technological society—brought many benefits in the fields of medicine, health, communications, and education for which we can all be thankful. However, the humanism and the social and economic upheaval also produced the spread of immorality on radio and in the movies. Never before could evil be broadcast, causing a dramatic change in millions of people's beliefs almost instantaneously. Of course, the same medium also carried evangelical messages of the gospel of Jesus Christ, which converted and comforted many who perhaps would have never been reached except by this means.

So the decade of the 1930s was a mix of blessings and curses, but it seems to be the decade when, because of these weaknesses and so-called advancements, we turned the corner and entered on a destructive path.

World War II

Few people would argue the justification for our participation in this war of the 1940s that sought to suppress totalitarianism and the reign of an antichrist dictator—Adolph Hitler. If there is such a thing as a just war, this was it. We were literally defending our own shores and families. Nevertheless, one of the things that occurred stateside during that war was the mass exodus of young American males when dads, husbands, sons, uncles, nephews, and cousins went off to fight, resulting in an even further breakup of the family.

Because many people were lonely, numerous marriages were entered into solely because of that loneliness. A here-today-gone-tomorrow mentality began to prevail as traditional courtships became rare. War weary fighting men—those who had not received a "Dear John" letter leaving them hurt and abandoned overseas—came home to a wife and sometimes a toddler or half-grown son that they did not know.

During the 1940s, however, many families had extra pressure and turmoil placed on them. God was still alive in the hearts of many Americans, and Sabbath worship and participation in a church community was still very much a part of our country's fabric. Most folks still wanted to be part of a family and church; however, the lyrics to popular wartime and post-wartime songs illustrate clearly how morality and godly proprieties were slipping away. Such lyrics would have been unacceptable even a few years before the war began. Agnosticism was becoming acceptable.

As war-struck families began to break up, there were more hurting people than we ever had in our entire history, which naturally resulted in more troubled kids. During that decade and the one that followed, we began seeing movies that depicted adultery, divorce, and fornication in a casual, flippant, and even comical vein.

Although the late 1940s brought a tremendous national prosperity that lasted for 25 years or more, as a nation, our focus was shifting from God and family to materialism and hedonism. The newly birthed psychoanalysis of the 1930s, with its atheistic underpinnings, began replacing confession and repentance for many. The psychoanalyst replaced friends, family members, ministers, priests, rabbis, and even God. People found a fatherly image in the countenance of Sigmund Freud. Of course, it was also in the late 1940s that television came along. The evil that could only be heard on radio could now be seen live on television. Being the mixed blessing that it was, TV also spread the Word of God in varying degrees through such men as Billy Graham and Bishop Fulton J. Sheen.

Alcohol consumption was also on the rise through the 1940s and 1950s, and drunkenness became laughable and acceptable on television and in the movies. To meet the need, Alcoholics Anonymous (A.A.), founded in the 1930s, came of age in the 1940s when it was approved by the American Medical Association. The A.A.

program and Big Book were based on biblical principles and a belief in God's extraordinary healing power. The principles remain, but the gospel is not central to the A.A. program.

Baby Boomers

During the materialistic decade of the 1950s, the baby boomers were subjected to the godlessness that had been creeping into our society during the previous two decades or more. There were more divorces than ever before, more materialism and immorality, more mobility and transience. Television and other media, which may not be inherently evil, can nevertheless be used as a tool for either good or evil. But not much good was coming out of television in the 1950s, and that fact hasn't changed till this day. Violence, sex, and abject materialism were vividly glorified and repeated so many times on the TV screen and in movies that many impressionable young minds began thinking that this was all there was to life. By the late 1950s, the Beat Generation appeared on the scene. Bohemianism, hedonism, alcohol and drug abuse, and sexual promiscuity were held up as increasingly acceptable lifestyles—justifiable expressions of rebellion against society and restrictive family upbringing.

In the 1950s, thanks to the mass media, children between the ages of 13 and 19 were no longer called children but teenagers. That developmental period of life,

once labeled and set apart, began having negative con-
notations, most of which had to do with teenagers' disobedience, rebellion, and unmanageability. A teenager
today is expected to behave in these odd ways and be
wild, contrary, and mildly unhappy. In the days when
the family was the family, the Bible was the Bible, and
God still knew best, teenagers were guided, trained, corrected, and loved while they were going through these
hormonal years. That was the time period when it was
especially important for parents to *train up their children in the way they should go so that when they get
old they will not depart from it.*

Did Parents Give Up?

Many parents gave in and stopped believing that God
was still on His throne and that the holy Bible was our
eternal owner's manual. Increasing numbers of busy parents and their troubled kids abdicated their God-given
seats of authority. Divorce caused many parents to be
absent from those seats of authority altogether.

During the 1960s and 1970s, television psychologists,
academes, cult leaders, and radical student activists
began telling parents what they ought to think and say.
Some told all parents to just go to hell. This period can
now be looked back upon as the time when parenthood
collapsed. No longer did the dog wag the tail. Parents
gave up their control. Juvenile delinquency has always
existed, but it wasn't until the early 1960s that drugs, al-

cohol, and street gangs in New York City and other large metropolitan areas gained worldwide attention, and youth rebellion became ingrained into the social fabric.

How were the 1960s and 1970s different from the rest of history? For one thing, many cultures used to usher a male child into manhood with some kind of a ceremony and celebration, The bar-mitzvah is an example of this rite of passage. Sadly, the mark of many emerging young men these days is more likely to be their rebellion against their fathers. Such rebelliousness today represents acceptability with peers, independence, and maturity. Love and honoring of one's parents has become antiquated and virtually prohibited since then for many children. In defense of the kids, I'll note that even the most "normal" and stable of them go through some degree of rebellion and testing of their parents. This is part of the maturation process. However, with some exceptions, the type and degree of rebellion we're seeing these days develops in homes where parents are failing in their God-given responsibilities as loving, nurturing, and disciplining adults.

In the 1970s, *Time* magazine boldly pronounced, "God Is Dead" on its cover. The issue carried a not completely accurate cover story depicting the exodus of churchgoers from the traditional enclaves of Christianity and showing how secular humanism and other philosophies were replacing God and religion. Supreme Court decisions throughout the 1960s and 1970s tossed God out of the classroom and tried to place Him in the back seat of our culture, behind the humanistic notions of freedom of choice and every man is a god.

Caveat

I need to inject here a caution about how I personally view the many changes our nation and society have undergone since the 1930s. In presenting this overview of how troubled kids get that way, I am simply describing the moral and spiritual decline of the family, the church, and society at large. This history is not intended to be detailed or complete, but has been capsulized to give one interpretation of how things got the way they are now. My presentation of this chronology of our spiritual decline is not an attempt to judge or fix blame on any individual or category of people such as fathers and mothers, academics, or others.

As Christians we are directed to hate sin but love sinners. We also believe there is an age-old battle between good and evil, one with which literature has been replete ever since man began to write—you know, the battle between the guys with the white hats and the ones with the black hats. It is the contest between sin (our lower nature) and righteousness (our godly essence). Our chief weapons are love, prayer, and the Word of God. Our victory comes in living out these things and walking the walk instead of just talking the talk. Our prayer is the same kind of prayer that Columbus spoke as he set out to discover the New World, the prayer of the Pilgrims who came to settle in our land, the prayer that declared our independence from England, and the prayer that opened and closed the Constitutional Convention. And it is the same kind of prayer that opened each school day for children before the morals of our country started really bottoming out.

The New Family

Every few years sociologists redefine the American family and come up with a variety of new configurations. It is difficult, although not impossible, to find the remnants of the American family as we knew it during the first half of this century, or even 25 years ago. That is how fast the institutions of marriage and the family have collapsed.

The U.S. census figures show that the percentage of children living in married-couple families decreased from 77 percent in 1980 to 69 percent in 2002.[9] One in three women giving birth is now unmarried, up from 5% in 1960. The proportion of children under 18 living in single parent families rose from 23% to 31% between 1980 and 2000, reflecting increased rates of both non-marital childbearing and divorce.

George Barna, author and president of the Barna Research Group, which surveys and interprets trends in American life, confirms what we already suspect—that progressively fewer wives are at home anymore. About 22% are waiting to greet their families at the end of the day, down from 61% three decades ago. Often both parents are working.

Other researches say that only 26% of American families are what we consider traditional, that is, having a biologically related mother, father, and children living under the same roof. This means that 74% of today's families are composed of partners who are remarried and stepchildren, or a single parent, usually the mother. About 80% of our Ranch Hope boys come from single parent homes.

Single Parents

Single parenthood is regrettably common in this decade. Close to 90% of single parents are women, and according to the Census Bureau, their numbers increased 41% in the 1980s. The single parents of our boys at Ranch Hope endure an extraordinary amount of stress and economic hardship. According to Mr. Barna's research, if the current trend continues, of all children born in 1990, six out of ten will live in a single parent home for some period before they are 18.[10] The single mother's stress, of course, is passed along to the children.

Grandparents are increasingly stepping in to fill the gap of the broken family, with more and more of them assuming the role of parents. According to *U.S. News and World Report*, 4% of all white children and 12% of all black children now live with their grandparents. About half of these are with both grandparents; the other half are only with their grandmas.[11] "Beyond them," says the magazine article, "are the millions of grandparents that have assumed important part-time child-rearing responsibilities because of the growth of single parent households and the number of families where both parents work."

What is the total number of kids, many of them dead-end kids, who are presently living with their grandparents? Citing U.S. Census Bureau figures, the article says the total is 3.2 million in the United States, an increase of almost 40% over the past decade. Those are the known figures, the article says, adding that "many who are now coming to grips with the trend fear that it could be three to four times worse than that. There is hardly a more frightening leading indicator of the devastation wrought by the nation's manifold social ills, and no class or race is immune."

Are grandmas and grandpas happy to be filling the role of parents? "Many of them are racked by shame and guilt at the fact that their own children have failed as parents, and many blame themselves, wondering where they've gone wrong as parents," the article says. It continues: "In order to provide a safe and loving home for their grandchildren, some of these grandparents must emotionally abandon their own abusive or drug-addicted children. The stresses are compounded by the fact that some of the children they inherit are among the most needy, most emotionally damaged, and most angry in the nation.

Chapter 5

The Legacy of Divorce

*N*ewsweek reports that 1970 was a watershed period in the history of American marriages. Before then, divorce was comparatively rare, and youngsters felt ashamed of their status as products of what were then called "broken homes."[12]

Over the 1970s, however, the divorce rate soared to a record high. In 1965, when Ranch Hope was just getting started, the divorce rate was 2.5 per 1,000 population; by 1976 it had doubled to 5.0. Through most of the 1970s and 1980s, there were 1.1 million divorces annually. A slight leveling off was seen in the late 1980s, perhaps because fewer couples were bothering to get married. In 1999, there was one divorce for every two marriages in the United States. (Since 1999, the government has stopped collecting marriage and divorce rates.[13]).

More than one million children are affected by divorce each year.[14] Instead of using the term, "broken homes," people label them as members of "single-parent households" and "blended families"—as though sanitized titles could hide the messy reality of families torn apart.

Even among families where there is no divorce, virtually every child and every adult knows at least one family that is broken by divorce. It's a condition that surrounds all of us. Second marriages are reported by experts to have an even higher failure rate. In fact, more people are part of second marriages today than first marriages. One quarter of all Americans have experienced at least one divorce.

Divorce in our own lives, in our peripheral family, or among friends, affects our relationships in many detrimental ways. It often unleashes a torrent of anger and other hurtful emotions from which psychologists say we rarely recover without long-term counseling or professional help. Most people don't get that help. Spouses and children from broken homes bring their emotional baggage with them, whether it is into another marriage, the workplace, or other relationships.

The legacy of divorce is so debilitating that major secular publications now devote entire cover stories to it. Sadly, George Barna's surveys indicate that most young adults now believe that divorce is an inevitable part of marriage. They marry hoping it will endure, "but expecting it to explode or dissolve. Not only that, we may be nearing a day when adults marry three times over the course of their lives: once during the first years in the work force as they set themselves up in a career and family; once during their years of achievement in business as their children leave the nest, and a third time when they are retired and need companionship."

Christians should not like to hear such statistics. Jesus exhorted us to not divorce our husbands or wives except, perhaps, if they commit adultery. It is sad that Christian couples too often break up under the guise of separation. The Greek word for divorce means to "separate" or "tear apart." That is why the *Amplified Bible* says, "The Lord hates divorce and marital separation" (Mal. 2:16). It notes the identical meaning of the two words. While there certainly are reasons to be married and separate for a season, the word "separation" can become a handy euphemism used by a partner who really has divorce in his or her heart.

Paul Meier, M.D., director of the Minirth-Meier Clinic's psychiatric and counseling centers, says that the 1980s was the decade of "disposable everything," and that sadly, "all too many still view marriage as disposable." He says, "If it doesn't work, we'll just bail out and get a divorce."[15]

Time Does Not Heal

Dr. Meier points out that it is only the old school of thought which held that divorce would affect children for awhile, but they would get over it. "More and more research seems to indicate that divorce is, in fact, devastating to children. The trauma of divorce follows throughout their lives. There are even adult children of divorce support groups springing up to help people deal with the residual pain experienced form their parents divorce."[16]

The predominant damaging experience of every child of divorce, Dr. Meier says, is grief. The child experiences both the loss of a balanced parental unit and the daily parental support he or she so badly needs. The child also experiences a loss of identity as his or her sense of security, financial future, lifestyle, and relationships change, often overnight. At the initial abandonment, a child of divorce can be thrust into a sort of emotional and spiritual shock as his fundamental security base abruptly disappears.

Our staff at Ranch Hope and leaders elsewhere in the field of psychology and counseling say that because divorced parents are licking their own emotional and spiritual wounds and trying to adjust to their own sense of loss, they often neglect the child's needs, failing to provide sufficient nurturing for the child who experiences a crushing loss of self-esteem.

Moreover, many experts say the emotional wounds of divorce, which we once believed healed themselves with time, often doggedly follow children into their adulthood, hampering their ability to develop close and meaningful relationships with other people. Some of the kids at Ranch Hope, who have divorced parents, develop a "peace-at-any-price style" of relating, which only lays the groundwork for future problems with codependency. We see this in the boy or girl who is the proverbial brown-noser or people-pleaser. They are yes men; yet, behind their outward attitude of cooperation and conciliation is tremendous rebellion and anger that will most likely one day be turned on themselves or others.

We have also discovered that our kids of divorce, while they might maintain a macho exterior are actually carrying deep internal wounds and painful feelings of sadness. Many children of divorce have a deep sense of loneliness and isolation and may also carry terrible feelings of guilt. Dr. Meier says that many children blame themselves and feel that somehow they could have prevented the divorce if only they had behaved better or just were not the person they are.

Dr. Barna says that offspring from broken homes are more likely to get divorced themselves, are less satisfied with lives, and are less apt to achieve high-status occupations.

At Ranch Hope, we believe that what God has joined together, no man or woman should tear asunder. Today it is evident to us that this divine command is being disobeyed by Christians and non-Christians alike on the largest scale since Christ walked the earth.

Divorce—whether physical or emotional—is one of the devil's primary strategies for destroying what we universally refer to as Christ's Church, the entire body of believers. By attacking and destroying the first human institution that God created—the family—the devil is able to bind the energy, the creativity, and fruitfulness of the people of God.

Referring to what many report as a lingering, almost unshakable guilt among those who have quickly and recklessly put aside their spouses, Dr. Meier concludes: "God does not arbitrarily give us instruction just to make us squirm. He does so because He knows that following His ways will result in a happier, more fulfilling life and that disobeying them will lead to unhappiness and misery."

As instruments of God's healing to dead-end kids, we see the misery firsthand as the legacy of divorce continuously shows up at our doorstep. Like a toxic oil spill in an already rolling sea, the polluting effects of divorce spread gradually, inevitably being dispersed far and wide, snuffing out life wherever it goes, and despoiling what God intended to be pristine.

Chapter 6

Other Influences
On Young People

Divorce is not the only cause for the hurt that resides in our children. There are other tragic situations, which are so significant that our facilities would still be full even if there were no divorces. These situations have to do with the so-called normal family life of those who do stay together.

More than half of married moms with children under the age of one are now in the labor force and are struggling to find safe, affordable child care. According to one report, most of these women "struggle to find safe affordable child care. Many child care situations do not provide a consistent care giver. And few day care centers can match the recommended ration of one worker for every three infants."[17]

It's not just Mom who is abandoning the children for a day. At about the time we were responding to God's call to establish Ranch Hope in the 1960s, sociologists began measuring how much time parents were spending with their kids because of the economic pressures being placed on our society's highly competitive work force. According to University of Maryland sociologist John Robinson, today's parents spend 40% less time with their children than did parents in 1965—from about 30 hours per week to 17 hours in 1998.[19] Emphasis on careers and material possessions along with stagnating wages, escalating taxes, and the increased cost of living, have played a major role in creating this parental absenteeism.

A survey reported by the University of Minnesota in 2002 stated that less than 1/3 of U.S. families say they eat dinner together most evenings, and of those, more than 1/2 said that they had the television on during that time. Meal time is no longer family time. Although troubled kids are the focus of what we call our national disgrace, the emotionally disturbed and neurologically impaired youth who end up at residential treatment centers and other custodial facilities are more likely an indicator of a condition that extends by lesser degrees into the entire spectrum of the youth population. For example, researchers say that Christian young people are now just as susceptible to drug and alcohol abuse as their non-Christian counterparts. Jim Burns, president of the National Institute of Youth Ministry in San Clemente, California, says that studies show that by the time Christian young people turn 18:

- 85% will have experimented with alcohol

- 57% will have tried an illicit drug

- 33% will smoke marijuana on occasion

- 33% will get drunk at least once a month

- 25% will smoke marijuana regularly

- 17% will have tried cocaine or crack[19]

Another study also shows that 35% of all high school seniors have had five or more drinks in a row at least once during any previous two-week period. For most 18 year olds, five or more drinks in a row should be considered "drunk as a skunk." According to the study, many of today's teens first used alcohol at age 12 and tried marijuana at age 13.

Another influence on the general youth population that intensified in the 1980s was music with a very oppressive and negative message with which hurting kids unfortunately readily identify. Many kids we have worked with seem to be particularly attracted to the heavy metal and black metal music that does not glorify God or His wondrous creation but instead glorifies doom and gloom, illicit sex, alcohol and drugs, unrequited love, painful romances, violence, suicide, and even Satan. We don't often come across the blatantly satanic in most of our kids. Nevertheless, we have had young people arrive with satanic and demonic symbols emblazoned on their sweatshirts and jackets, and sometimes they bring cassettes of heavy metal and black metal music. All these things, of course, are either confiscated and held or sent home.

Satan is a rebellious high angel and the archenemy of all righteousness—a perfect symbol for troubled and rebellious kids to emulate. Many parents tolerate this kind of music as well as satanic practices and rituals, thinking it's just another fad their youngster is going through. Teenagers today are growing up in a culture replete with satanic symbols and subliminal messages. In addition to the music, there are demonic video games and toys, horror movies, and occult games and emblems. Some parents I've talked to mistakenly believe it's all very harmless and that their kids will one day grow out of it. With names like Slayer, Megadeath, Mettalica, and Venom, black metal rock groups are actually preaching an antichrist gospel of despair with their music, which laughs at authority and applauds the spirit of darkness and death. Even those who mistakenly do not even believe that Satan exists and can influence their lives on earth from his dark spiritual realm must ask themselves why we would want to expose our impressionable and vulnerable children to such a dark, desperate, and destructive message.

Thankfully, there is an abundance of good Christian music available, providing an alternative to this kind of garbage for those kids who have been taught that there is a difference. We encourage Christian kids to listen to uplifting and positive music that glorifies Christ and His creation, and affirms life and eternity rather than death and damnation.

Only slightly removed from the extreme of black and heavy metal music is an entire gamut of popular music that, if you listen carefully, is almost as bad. Most pop music extols sexual prowess, promiscuity, and getting "high." It laments broken love affairs, jilted lovers, and sings of romance in plaintive tones that can easily be mistaken for depression, major indigestion, or a badly stubbed toe. Pop music dominates the music market of our young people. Only recently our culture has come to grips with "rap music.' More and more leaders are showing concern about the lyrics.

If this is love, then let me out of here. The Word of God gives us the true definition of love in I Corinthians 13. Among other things, love is patient, kind, and enduring, not angry. It does not seek to be right all the time and allows us to rise above ourselves. Real love is gentle. I was thinking of the passage recently after going through the TV listings for the week of Valentine's Day, our national celebration of love. The highlighted movie for that evening was, *I Love You to Death*, which was profiled like this: "The wife of an unfaithful man tries to kill him several times, with lots of help, and he still doesn't die."[20] I thought to myself, *how cheerful! Really makes me want to tune in.*

My point is that children today are being given a distorted, anti-Christian definition of love by the media. Their definition is the antithesis of Jesus' selfless, sacrificial love and the way in which He loved the Church. Kids are buying the media's version because they haven't seen Christ's love modeled in the home, neighborhood, or media. Left alone to their own devices, whether in the house or on the streets, the minds of our as yet undisciplined and lonely kids search for diversion and wind up devising mischief CBS's *60 Minutes* featured a segment titled "Bang, You're Dead," which told of the hundreds of children shot dead or maimed with guns each year by other kids, mostly by accident or ignorance. Left at home alone, these children have access to 200 million guns in this country, 66 million of which are hand guns.

The question is, what are we armed against? How fearful and angry are we that we must be prepared to defend ourselves to death against an event, which for most of us rarely occurs? Could the answer be that our unrepented transgressions against our spouses and children, generation after generation, have put us under a curse of fear, lingering guilt, anger, or even paranoia? I am not questioning our constitutional right to bear arms. I am asking—against whom are we bearing arms? Has the way we have sinned in our hearts and lives against our marital partners, our children, and others left us open to the anger, violence, and revenge of the evil one? Perhaps, as a nation, we are convicted in our hearts by God of the tragedy we have wrought. The price we're paying is the emotional and physical death of our families and what the experts tell us is that lingering feeling that we just didn't do right by them.

Our nation is paying an even greater price for what author and psychologist Dr. Charles R. Solomon has called the rejection syndrome.[21] It happens when we feel unloved and unaccepted by others, Solomon says, so we deliberately or unwittingly pass rejection on to others. According to Solomon it is "one of the most destructive forces on earth today." In his book *The Rejection Syndrome: The Need for Genuine Love and Acceptance,* he states, "Those who have no relationship with the Lord Jesus Christ have no support system to heal the hurts which a rejecting society has dealt them. These hurts and rejections are passed on to others through frustration, hostility, and anti-social behavior, sometimes including violence."

About half the young people that come to Ranch Hope have been either physically or sexually abused. According to *Philadelphia Inquirer* columnist Claude Lewis, "There are 500,000 such cases that take place each year in our nation. These are just the cases we know of," he writes.[22] This abuse is usually committed by family members, friends, or other relatives who were once (and may still be) hurting kids themselves. "A nation that fails to protect its young should never be called civilized," Lewis wrote. He went on to say, "The abuse of anyone is bad enough, but to allow helpless children to become victims is more a scandal against America than it is against any deeply troubled or impoverished family."

The scandal is reaping other evil dividends in many

cities and suburbs and causing a heightened crisis in our classrooms. ABC's *20/20* aired a segment titled "Teach at Your Own Risk."[23] This show reported on students and their parents attacking teachers in the schools, injuring them and sometimes maiming them for life. Hurt, which has turned to hatred, causes them to strike out at their teachers who are the authority figures that subconsciously remind them of their parents, according to the televised report. The United Federation of Teachers is so alarmed at the recent escalation of attacks that in some school districts it has set up teacher support programs that include self-defense in order to help them face violence in the classroom.

According to *20/20*, a 17-year-old assailant received a 5-15 year prison sentence for beating his teacher with a baseball bat and disabling and disfiguring him for life. The teacher can no longer teach. New York teachers claim that the schools have become "very dangerous places" and that "for all intents and purposes the streets are invading the schools."

Ranch Hope is ordained to be a center of prevention for this kind of violence by providing a disciplined, structured, and loving environment where kids don't have to fight or strike out. When they do, they pay an immediate price, as we'll see later on. Negative behavior is not met by violence here. We believe that the biblical admonition to use the rod on a child applies only to his parents and was meant to be applied consistently and lovingly during his formative years as a last resort. It was to be the final deterrent to severe rebellion and disobedience.

By the time young people arrive here, many times they have not been lovingly corrected by his parents, and sometimes they have been abused. The use of the rod by strangers who are trying to teach him a new and nonviolent way of life through Jesus would be counterproductive in most cases. Hurting kids generally don't need another hurt laid on them.

God's Timing

Violence, anger, and rejection are the archenemies that Ranch Hope was created to conquer. It was no coincidence that our arrival on the scene was in the 1960s, the decade by which all others are now compared. It was during the 1960s that Americans began turning away en masse from our Judeo-Christian morals and practices, and God began to be replaced in many people's hearts by secular humanism.

The 1960s was the decade when we decided that spending time in the office or earning overtime at the plant was better than spending time with junior or sis. It was when junior and sis began to rebel and decided that their parents were an embarrassment to be put down and scorned. It was when divorce was increasing into the mass sin it became in 1970. It was when juvenile delinquency took on crisis proportions. No coincidence, indeed. God knew exactly what He was doing; it's just that I didn't. I knew I was called to provide a home for troubled boys, but I never imagined that in 1999, law enforcement officers would arrest an estimated 2.5 million juveniles. Approximately 104,000 of these arrests were for violent crimes, and the most common offense was larceny-theft. The overall delinquency caseload was 48% larger in 1997 than it was in 1988, and an astounding 400% as large as it was in 1960.

In Chapter 3 we left off where I was waiting to hear from the Lord about continuing with Ranch Hope. I knew that He had ordained it, but I was looking for confirmation that I, Dave Bailey, should continue it. Little did I realize then that Ranch Hope was destined to become an embodiment of Christ's first century church—a community of believers doing the Lord's work and carrying out the Great Commission. During those early years as I waited to hear from the Lord, I walked by faith not by sight. The Lord had clearly shown me the need, but I was surrounded by negativism and sometimes felt like Job, with well-meaning but critical friends who were not helpful at all. I thank God for the ones who stood by me, however, and I especially thank Him for giving me the strength and courage to continue on.

Chapter 7

Some Early Miracles
and Mess Ups!

After asking the Lord for a sign that He wanted me to continue with the work of Ranch Hope, I was overjoyed when I received a swift response. Two days after my prayer in the shambles of the half-completed building, we were approved for a $25,000 grant to resume construction. Some might say that the approval of a grant we had applied for was neither a miracle nor an answered prayer. But when you realize that the application was no more than a shot in the dark that we took with the Turrell Foundation, a prestigious organization in New Jersey set up specifically for helping troubled children, the story takes on a more miraculous tone. You see, the Turrell Foundation usually required proof of a definite program in an established home with a proven track record. We met none of these criteria, and we were never even asked if we did. In the world of children's homes, we not only were the new kid on the block, we were disorganized and almost insolvent. If we had a specific program for treating troubled youth, it would have been news to everyone at Ranch Hope. So the grant was providential indeed. God gave us that $28,000.

About the same time the plague of incompetent tradesmen was lifted from us when the Lord sent us a master carpenter (sound familiar?), who along with my brother Pip, remained faithfully and consistently employed at the ranch for the next year. They completed the first building. What a blessing! Ranch Hope was back on its feet again. Nevertheless I knew that these wonderful developments, as meaningful as they were, would not absolve me of my responsibility to determine why the mission of Ranch Hope was failing. After all, the sad fact was that even the so-called nice boys who came here, the ones others called cream puffs, weren't responding positively to life at the ranch.

For one thing, my fresh-air philosophy of healing was collapsing before my very eyes. For example, I was being made painfully aware that you simply couldn't take a youth from the projects, put him in lie country, and expect him to be healed solely through religion and right living. More was needed. The city couldn't be taken out of the young person too abruptly.

One evening I went down to the cottage for a bed check at 2:30 a.m. and found Jerome, a 16-year-old from

Newark, wide awake and very unhappy. Mustering up my severest tone, I asked why he was still awake. "Them damn frogs," he barked. "Can't get to sleep 'cause o' them damn frogs." Jerome, of course, was referring to the melodious chorus of spring peepers that occurs each year. Being a country boy, I had a tough time at first accepting Jerome's protest, but I soon understood, however, that a city boy could find a chorus of frogs as annoying at bedtime as I would find the summer sounds of buses and people arguing out on the street if I were visiting his urban neighborhood for the first time. I had a lot to learn.

We discovered that bringing a city boy to Salem County, New Jersey, was a form of culture shock, like suddenly stepping off an airplane and being in Siberia for the first time. The boys needed more support and sympathy and a better period of acclimation before they could begin to benefit from the healing balm of country living. In some cases the boys absolutely could not adapt to the ranch, and these became our runaways.

Learning about country living came harder for some boys than others. For instance, the ranch once received several hundred tree seedlings free of charge—pines and hardwoods. I was in charge of planting this valuable landscaping gift, which we could never have afforded to buy. I gave one of the kids, Raul, about 30 of the seedlings, instructed him on exactly how to plant them in small holes, and left him alone in a corner of the ranch to do his planting. When Raul announced after just a short time that he was finished, I hiked over to his plot thinking something must be wrong. It was. Raul, being a foreigner to patience, obedience, and hard work, had dumped all 30 of the little trees in a hole and covered them almost completely with soil. Raul did not have a green thumb. In fact, he did not understand how things grow at all. Young people like Raul were fascinated by farm work—they could watch me do it for hours.

Team "Spirits"

I soon found that I couldn't *tell* these kids to do anything pertaining to nature or outdoor work. Detailed instruction and supervision were necessary for something as simple as mowing the lawn. Another thing I found out was that I could not expect dysfunctional kids who had never been seriously supervised by anyone and who had major ego problems to suddenly learn how to play team sports. Their idea of tough football ended up being similar to a gang war. If you were an offensive lineman, for instance, why block your opponent with your shoulders when a punch on the side of his head would drop him right away? Talk about offensive!

Also, there was no such thing as having one quarterback. If there were five guys on a team, there were five quarterbacks. The guy who yelled the loudest and slapped faces the hardest got to actually call the play—unless, of course, there was a more serious disagreement, in which case the game would end in a bloody huddle. My position as referee required a new job description—that of bouncer.

Speaking of bouncers, basketball progressed along somewhat similar lines. Why jump and block a good shot with your arm, the boys reasoned, when you could wrestle down the player in mid-air and rip the ball out of his hands? This was the first time I ever saw a boy tackled while taking a free shot at the foul line. It was not pretty. In fact, all team sports, as I knew them, eventually had to be not merely supervised but intervened upon. The games caused me to see team spirit in a whole new light, if you get what I mean.

In a more serious vein, it was at first a sad realization that these boys' natural, God-given proclivity for play—something that even creatures of the woods don't need to be taught—had been terribly distorted at home and on the streets. Clean competition and a sense of fair play were totally foreign to many of them. In the environments they came from, competition meant fighting for emotional and even physical survival. A sense of fair play is impossible to develop on your own if in your formative years you've been taught to distrust those closest to you—your mother, father, brother, sister, or other extended family members.

Don't Say You Love Me!

It was apparent, too, that some kids coming to the

Ranch were never truly loved by anyone or never allowed themselves to be loved. One day as I was trying to reprimand and encourage a 15-year-old named Dan, I said, "Do you know why you are able to be here on probation, why we have this ranch in the first place, and all these people are here to help you? It's because we love you." I was both grieved and astounded when Dan thought that I was making a homosexual overture. In his blessed but confused mind, he thought that a man who told a boy he loved him must be gay, which obviously is not true. A kid named Jeff told me, "Don't give me that love stuff. My father said he loved me, and he beat me. My mother used to say she loved me too, and she left me. Don't give me that love stuff."

Stick 'Em Up, Rev!

In addition to the boys, some of our early house parents also had serious problems, which became obvious one evening when I was frantically summoned to one of the cottages. Two house fathers had gotten into a fight and were about to go at each other just as I arrived. I was able to quell that situation. Another time, though, one of the house parents was fighting with his wife. When I arrived on the scene, dishes and glasses were shattering all over the place. The husband went into his room and shocked everyone by emerging with a pistol. "I'm gonna kill her or I'm gonna kill you," he said, as he jammed a cartridge into the handle of the gun, ready to fire. He pointed the gun at me and said, "Get out of here, she's gonna die." Well, I didn't leave. The Lord gave me the right words to dissuade him from the murder or perhaps the double murder. After what seemed like an eternity of talking and hoping he wouldn't kill me, he laid the gun down, and we all prayed together. He stayed on at the ranch for a short time but then left. The unfortunate thing was that the boys were listening to all this outside the door.

These house parents ultimately told me that they felt as though they had been placed under too much pressure through the long hours and too few days off. Some had simply cracked under the strain. This was yet another area where the ranch was failing. Furthermore, although the Lord had begun to show us His faithfulness, the ranch was by that time almost collapsing under the strain of the preceding years of experimentation and poor income. The time for experimentation was over. We needed to put in place a well-defined program and a plan of operation, and we needed to do it fast because our failure rate was a deplorable 80%.

On the Road

Eileen and I decided to examine and reevaluate every aspect of Ranch Hope. We packed the car and embarked on a 4-week trip to every boys home we had ever heard about and compared notes on each. We went to Starr Commonwealth in Michigan, founded by Floyd Starr, who gave us great courage to continue. We visited the Missouri Home for Boys, whose director began our conversation with, "Reverend, whatever possessed you to get into this business?" He had plenty of negatives for me, and I needed to hear them.

Interestingly enough, Boys Town, the world-renowned home for troubled boys, was not what we wanted for Ranch Hope. It was so large we couldn't relate to it. They accommodated all sorts of kids, including orphans. While we were there, the officials were making plans to begin accepting girls. Boys Town, of course, does have a marvelous ministry, which even includes taking in hearing and speaking impaired children. We also went to Cal Farley's Boys Ranch in Texas, which had 400 kids at that time. We learned a lot on this trip that we wanted to incorporate when we returned.

Out in the Cold

Only a few years after starting Ranch Hope, I joyfully discovered that local Methodist churches and pastors were very supportive of our work. Although I had no reason to believe that the Methodist Conference of Southern New Jersey would feel any differently, I took the parting advice of my pastor at Pitman Methodist Church and sought the official support and guidance of the bishop in Philadelphia. Although I arrived on time for my appointment with the bishop after an hour's drive, I was left to languish in the waiting room of his office for another hour. Before I even saw him, I was beginning to get a feeling for what his leaning would be. Our meeting consisted of a ten-minute dissertation from the bishop, who did all he could to discourage me by going through the laundry list of all the negatives I had been hearing from the secular world all along—the ranch will be a very expensive ordeal; the problems of the boys will overwhelm me; I should stick to being a pastor in a local church.

Afterwards, although I was allowed to keep my nominal affiliation with the Conference and the Methodist Church, I lost my status as a minister, along with all housing, retirement, and hospitalization benefits. I continued to be certain, however, that my vision for helping troubled boys was from God. From that day when I met with the bishop in 1963, it was 17 years before I was taken back under the wing of the Methodist Church. I understand, however, that the bishop was preoccupied with his duties, and I blame neither him nor the church hierarchy for the separation. This lack of interest by my own denomination was merely another obstacle that had to be dealt with, another rugged mountain that taught me to have hind's feet on high places. Perhaps the growth and expansion of the ranch might have come too easily if I had received the early enthusiastic support of the church. It certainly would have made fund-raising easier.

I always had an abiding faith that the Ranch was doing the work of Jesus Christ by bringing light into this world. It was the Church in action and the gates of hell would not prevail against it. Satan had his way in this one area of Ranch Hope for 17 years, but after being resisted for so long by the power of Christ in His people, he finally had to let go. When we resist the devil, as the Bible says, he will ultimately flee.

In the early 1980s, unbeknownst to me, a minister friend in another part of the state, Lloyd Applegate, had been doing some behind-the-scenes petitioning for me among the conference membership, asking why I should not be readmitted. After all, he reasoned, Reverend Bailey had continued ministering as an evangelist, has held regular Methodist services, has taught Sunday school, and has had the Ranch Hope gospel singing group give concerts in Methodist churches during all 17 years. When I finally got to talk to some district superintendents of the church at a meeting, one of them asked, "Dave, why did you ever leave the Conference years ago?" My answer was, "I never left the Conference, the Conference left me," Shortly thereafter the Ranch became an "advanced special," a classification that allowed churches to give to us as a missionary project. My relationship with the Conference has been excellent ever since. I knew someday it would all work out, for our God is a God of reconciliation.

Gaining in Wisdom and Knowledge

After the first four or five years, through our travels to other homes and by walking through our many weaknesses where God wanted to make us strong, the Lord finally had me growing in knowledge and wisdom. He is a truly rewarder of those who persevere. There is a line in an old song that says, "We should be careful not to give up just before our miracle arrives." We didn't give up.

Those early years showed us that success required not only a good and righteous people at the Ranch but also a good plan. We knew we had to establish a structured program and not allow the young people to just dangle in the wind. First, we had to have a better screening process whereby criminally violent boys who were absolutely incorrigible were kept out. Those with problems that could only be dealt with in a protective psychiatric setting were also screened out.

Ranch Hope has no bars on its windows and no walls or barbed wire to keep its precious residents inside. It was unfair, we decided, to expose boys who could be helped, or the surrounding community, to the potentially dangerous behavior of boys convicted of serious crimes. Ranch Hope was determined to be preventative, rehabilitative, and redemptive. We were not a correctional center or secured psychiatric facility. That was not in our calling. We were a residential treatment facility for the 98% of troubled boys who did not use guns or knives, or commit acts of violence. We couldn't handle that other 2% and vowed to employ a better screening process to protect our residents as well as encouraging authorities to see that the very violent youth could get help at the appropriate facilities.

Moreover, as the mission of the ranch developed more clearly and we began to focus on a specific program, we realized that our purpose was to intervene in the lives of young people before they got into serious trouble. We began emphasizing three areas of need—home difficulties, school difficulties, and community difficulties. We use the term *troubled* to avoid the stigma of terms such as *delinquent*. Indeed, they are troubled. We found, however, that if Ranch Hope properly intervened early on, many of these young people could, with God's grace, be turned around. They could actually begin striving for something that was totally new to them: a meaningful, productive life, free of the courts and periodic or permanent incarceration.

Chapter 8

When God Moves
Into the Neighborhood

The Ranch Hope Campus in Alloway is presently a well-established and growing community of about 70 young people and over 100 full and part-time staffers. (Later we will discuss our additional campuses and ministries.) As the aerial photo at the end of the following photo section illustrates, we have 15 buildings on 135 pastoral acres with rich woodlands and a beautiful lake. I am told that the old abandoned farm we purchased in the early '60s for $18,600 is now worth something like $2.5 million. Hundreds of boys and girls have come through Ranch Hope and gone on to live meaningful, productive lives.

Our campus is laid out in a sort of a semicircle. Standing at the base of that semicircle, one faces the chapel, parking lot, and administration building. Behind them, around the periphery of the semicircle, are from left to right: our Strang School (named after the previously mentioned benefactor, Hiram Strang); Retzlaff Gym, named after the former Philadelphia Eagle football star Pete Retzlaff; and the Mike Schmidt Baseball Field, named after the former Philadelphia Phillies third baseman. Then there are five cottages and the cafetorium—the building that serves as both our cafeteria and small auditorium. The ranch houses or cottages are sprawling one-story structures that each house eight youth and their house parents and family in an adjoining apartment Each building has an activity room for television and games, as well as the bedrooms. The central campus is dissected by a narrow creek with a small footbridge connecting the school sector with the living sector, and together they make up our neighborhood.

I would like you to get a better feel for the ranch through the words of Val Quakenbush, a special education teacher who felt moved to write about her observations in one of our local newspapers. Her story, briefly edited here, provides a good sense of Ranch Hope.

> As I enter the Ranch Hope campus, I pass a sign that reads, "Children at Play." The first two times, I wondered how the streetwise young residents would feel about being called children.

> Then I began to pay closer attention. I saw inner city kids gleefully beg the principal to repeat a magic trick. I saw barefooted boys racing across

90

campus to the swimming pool on a hot summer day. I saw some fishing and others enjoying a game of kickball with their house parents.

I saw boys who had been dismissed as classroom deadwood get excited about learning and achieving good grades. I came to the conclusion that the term "children" was appropriate—these boys were regaining a childhood that had almost been stolen from them by poverty, drugs, crime-filled streets, or parents too young to have children.

The Ranch Hope program, inspired by Romans 15:1 ("We then that are strong ought to bear the infirmities of the weak, and not to please ourselves") consists of three components—home life, school, and counseling. The backbone of the program is the point/rank system, which enables a boy to earn more privileges as he earns points and progresses in rank. A "ranch hand," for instance, is eligible to make trips off campus with house parents or to have a 10-hour weekend pass to leave campus with a house parent, school staff, or responsible adult. "Stars" are eligible for monthly field trips and 48-hour weekend passes. In addition to the privileges assigned to rank, there are many school field trips which serve as incentives for good grades or good behavior.

Another component of the program is the chapel, presided over by a chaplain. Although the young people don't have religion "crammed down their throats," weekly chapel services are held and they are encouraged to attend and participate in the services. The chapel service is also remedial, with everything geared to reach troubled youth."

Let me add to Val's observations that weekly prayer breakfasts are held for the staff. These are often led by our chaplain and myself. Three different meetings are held each week so all the departments of the staff can participate.

Spiritual Foundations

Romans 15:1, mentioned earlier, is at the heart of our Christian walk. It expresses Christ's core message that we love our neighbors as ourselves. Many Christians pay too little heed to the love yourself part of this great commandment. Loving ourselves, far from what we might interpret as conceit or self pride, goes hand in hand with loving others. We've found at Ranch Hope that troubled youth often have extremely low self-esteem with little regard for themselves and others. A healthy self-esteem and right standing with God, which is necessary for them to love themselves, has often been blocked by an ungodly upbringing. They have a basic distrust of adults because of being emotionally, sexually, and physically abused or abandoned by the adults in their lives. Our central goal is to bear the youths' infirmities, to love them, to restore their self-esteem, and have them, if they so choose, open their heart to the love of God. Simply stated, our mission is R & R—rehabilitation and redemption. One of our mottoes is, "The youth comes first."

We believe the Word of God, as expressed by Paul in Romans 8:35, that says nothing (including a highly dysfunctional upbringing or abusive childhood) can separate us from God's love. Nothing! The thing we call grace, which is God's unmerited and unconditional love, is available to all His children—both the good ones and the bad ones—if they are open to receive it. At Ranch Hope we try to provide the spiritual climate and emotional soil for boys and girls to accept the Lord into their hearts, an act that can enhance their progress and prepare the way for miraculous healing and recovery.

The greatest healing that occurs comes through this spiritual aspect combined with specific therapeutic and behavior modification methods widely accepted as effective by the secular world. Our approach is not a hardnosed brand of evangelism. Life in the new millennium is too complex for a legalistic religious philosophy of recovery. While there is discipline, the Ranch Hope formula, if I may call it that, is not a rigidly structured program that forces any particular religion or denomination on a boy as a condition of his recovery. First, we couldn't do that if we wanted to; and second, we are wise enough to know that, as our detective friend from the state police told us, "You can't jam Jesus down these boys' throats. It doesn't work."

The Family

In ministering Christ's love and comfort, the Ranch seeks to replicate the nuclear family, which, according to Ephesians 3:14-15, is the basic social unit of Christ's Kingdom. As we saw in earlier chapters, the widespread alienation, anger, and rebelliousness of today's young people is directly related, and historically traceable to the dissolution of the traditional nuclear family as ordained by God. Without a sense of belonging, without the blessing of a godly home life, children easily become less than the Lord intended, wandering aimlessly into a life of giving and receiving hurt and pain.

If Ranch Hope has a special anointing, it is its call for replicating the family. In an age when a true family environment in residential treatment is almost unheard of, we have been blessed with mothers and fathers on the staff along with their own children who settle in to make Ranch Hope their own permanent home. They spiritually adopt another eight or more boys with whom they live 24 hours a day. Many secular treatment homes have found this increasingly impossible. The strength and commitment needed to raise one's family in a kind of fish bowl, for all to see, is almost impossible without one's life being dedicated to and empowered by Christ. While the secular homes for troubled boys have house parents who may or may not be married and who usually work a regular eight-hour shift, our parents don't have to go home at the end of the day because they are home. Of course, we do employ child care workers who work regular schedules here but live off the ranch and return to their families at night. There is considerable stress on our house parents, but through their own support network and counseling they truly believe, as I do, that we can do all things through Christ who strengthens us. His mercies are new every day, and His grace is sufficient to see us through.

More than 80% of Ranch Hope children are from broken or non-traditional homes with one parent. Many boys and girls have been abused physically, emotionally, or sexually, and some come to us from another institution, either another rehabilitation facility, juvenile shelters, or detention centers where they have shown promise of improving. Some come to us from foster group homes where they were too disruptive to remain.

The circumstances from which they all come are not what the Lord meant when He said to "train a child in the way he should go, and when he is old he will not turn from it" (Prov. 22:6). Often the parents of these boys and girls have paid no heed to the biblical admonition against frustrating their children or provoking them to anger (Col. 3:21). At the Ranch, however, every new boy encounters a house that becomes his home. The door to his house parents' apartment on the same floor is never closed to them. They are almost always available there or close by on the campus. Usually this extended family is composed of eight boys and the child-care workers—sometimes up to a dozen altogether.

Spiritual Adoption

Young people are referred to Ranch Hope by school boards, by judges who recommend residential treatment, and by caseworkers with the New Jersey State Division of Youth and Family Services (DYFS). Although 80% of the support for the boys and girls comes from the state, we are not mandated to take anyone. In some cases, young people may be sent here because they have no parents or no peripheral family member to take them in. No one just arrives here and takes up residency. Case files ar- rive first and are examined by our admission and review committee, which is made up of the ranch director, a psychologist, the residential administrator, the school administrator, a social services administrator, and at least one childcare worker.

If the young people's background suggests they are potential candidates for Ranch Hope, they will come here for a three-to-five day pre-placement evaluation by the committee. During this period, they become actual residents and are observed, interviewed, and evaluated by house parents and the rest of the staff at the admissions and review committee's weekly meeting on Wednesday afternoon. Of course, Ranch Hope does not in any way *legally* adopt a child at all, but in a manner of speaking, the admissions and review determination is actually a decision to *spiritually* adopt them based on whether they would benefit from living here and have proven to be compatible with the others who are generally receptive to being helped. Keep in mind that ours is a long-term treatment. It is only effective if the child stays at least 18 months to two years or more. He must have time to settle into his new home and become secure in knowing that the people here will not abandon him physically or emotionally. One of the benefits of a real home life is that it is a relatively permanent existence in which you can trust the family members. This trust and security takes time.

Seven Needs

I believe that all children have seven basic needs. The degree to which these needs are met determines how troubled and hurt or how healthy a child will become. First, they need *status*. I'm not necessarily talking about giving them fancy clothes and a 21-speed bike. However, they must feel that they count for something, that they are important.

Security is the second need. Boys and girls at Ranch Hope need to know they have a future and their lives are hopeful.

Next, they need *acceptance* and to feel approved of wherever they are in life. Often these boys and girls have been constantly criticized and rejected.

The fourth need is *love*, pure and simple. I call your attention to the classic definition of love found in First Corinthians 13. I like the translation of the Amplified Bible best:

Love for Dead-End Kids

Love endures long and is patient and kind; love never is envious nor boils over with jealousy, is not boastful or vainglorious, does not display itself haughtily. It is not conceited [arrogant and inflated with pride]; *it is not rude* [unmannerly] *and does not act unbecomingly. Love* [God's love in us] *does not insist on its own rights or its own way, for it is not self-seeking; it is not touchy or fretful or resentful; it takes no account of the evil done to it* [it pays no attention to a suffered wrong].

It does not rejoice at injustice and unrighteousness, but rejoices when right and truth prevail.

Love bears up under anything and everything that comes, is ever ready to believe the best of every person, its hopes are fadeless under all circumstances, and it endures everything [without weakening,

Love never fails [never fades out or becomes obsolete or comes to an end].

Of course it is not an easy thing to love as the Bible instructs. Being human, and by definition susceptible to sin and in a state of imperfection, we all fall short of the glory of God. I'm glad, though, that we Christians have a solid, authoritative definition to emulate. We take the above verses seriously, emphasizing *agape*, which in Greek means "an merited love"—love for the unlovable. Our young people need to be loved and to love.

The next need is *praise*, which to us means encouragement and support. We try to always acknowledge them for their progress and the good they do.

Discipline at the Ranch, which is the sixth need, is really teaching the order and self-control that the Word of God calls for in our lives. As responsible adults, we must set limits on their behavior and their privileges. Equally important is that those limits and the non-physical punishments meted out must be consistent. (Some child rearing experts even say that it's almost better for discipline to be consistently unfair rather than inconsistent and therefore confusing and upsetting to the youngster.)

We've saved the most important one for last—*God* is the seventh need. When young people with damaged and painful backgrounds arrive here, it is obvious to them that we are a Christian facility. They are surrounded by the Christ-centered lifestyle yet never overwhelmed by it. That is because we accept children of all races, creeds, and religions. We provide opportunities for them to attend services off campus if they are of other faiths. It does not work to jam Jesus down anyone's throat at any age.

Christ's bid to follow Him constituted a religion of attraction and spontaneity. A key message of His ministry on earth was one of freedom from the oppressive religiosity and forced devotion to dogma. Jesus spoke against this feigned spirituality practiced by the Pharisees and chief priests. The Pharisees failed to comprehend the gist of Jesus' life, which was to liberate man's spirit from the religiosity and legalism of the day. Jesus is never seen in Scripture as force-feeding His message. He wished His followers to discover freedom and joy by choosing His path. I never make apologies for the fact that the Ranch is centered in Jesus Christ. Some people have been offended by the cross in our logo, and a few years ago, because the number of referrals from local school boards and the state was increasing, a couple of school superintendents actually asked us to remove the cross from our logo. After some heated discussion, I simply told them, "No way!"

Through confrontations such as this, we have proven that our program and methods of counseling and therapy are acceptable by secular standards. Even the state has had to recognize that we are godly people concerned about young people.

Our staff is well aware that most new arrivals at Ranch Hope are in such distress that they have a tough time acclimating to this strange new environment Religion and spirituality are generally foreign to them. Although we believe that God already has each one's interests in mind by virtue of the fact that they arrived at our door, we busily address his other needs while making the Lord available to him at any time.

The Program

The Ranch Hope Point/Ranch system is our very

own version of the classic token economics approach to behavior modification. If that sounds like a mouthful, please understand that we are merely talking about a plan of consequences, both positive and negative. Points are assigned to just about everything boys or girls say and do here. In the course of a week, there are about 1200 points they can earn. Properly taking care of personal hygiene and appearance, for example, can earn 10 points each day. A young person can lose 50 points by cursing at a staff member or 200 points for fighting with someone. The point system is in effect every hour of the day, and there are two separate ones—one for school life and the other for home life in the cottages. New young people enter with the rank of "new ranch hands." As they consistently earn enough points each week, they are promoted to "ranch hands," then "star ranch hands," and finally "honor ranch hands." From the minute they open their eyes in the morning, they are earning or losing points for getting out of bed within five minutes, for showing up on time throughout the day, for the way they speak and relate to their peers and the staff, for doing their chores and schoolwork, and finally, for observing the quiet hour before retiring at night.

In addition to the points and ranks in school and in the cottages, they are rated from 0 to 3 for their level of participation and cooperation in regular group therapy sessions. If they are disruptive or fall asleep, points are deducted. In this way they are motivated to be proactive in their own wellness and rehabilitation. Finally, they are rated for how well they follow their individual treatment plan, which can include keeping a diary of their thoughts and speech when they're angry. This is an effective exercise meant to let them see how thoughts and feelings can result in violent or otherwise rebellious and disruptive behavior.

The set goal of a severely disturbed child in treatment might be simply to take care of his hygiene and appearance, which can be a major undertaking. Have you ever tried to get a house cat to get into the water? If you have, you can imagine what it is like to get some boys to shower regularly! They treat it like some form of punishment. We actually have to teach them how to stay clean and neat. Of course, the part all of them like best is the privileges they can earn!

The points each boy or girl accumulates during the week are placed in a bank account of sorts that they can draw from when a special off-campus trip or other activity comes up, or if they want to buy some approved item. They can make from four to six dollars a week, but there is no access to the money if they don't maintain a good record of points and ratings!

Privileges also include such things as joining clubs, using a skateboard on campus, weekly trips, visits home, having radios, making phone calls, and various crafts in which they can participate. Altogether there are 51 separate privileges at Ranch Hope.

Omar's Story

I recall a 14-year-old boy named Omar, who rather quickly reached the rank of star ranch hand, although he continued to have a problem intimidating other boys. Small in stature but with a rugged look, Omar used threats to get his way, something that could have been expected from a kid whose life had been spent mostly on the streets while his prostitute mother entertained a string of visitors in her bedroom. As a result of being pushed and ordered around by older and bigger kids on the street, as well as his mother, Omar developed a rock-hard wall of defensiveness. When he came to the Ranch, anyone he perceived as a threat got threatened, complete with Omar's vile cursing.

One spring weekend the staff and boys had planned a trip to the Philadelphia Zoo. Omar had never seen an animal more exotic than a dog, cat, or rat except on television. He was really excited about going, had plenty of spending money in his account, and an extra $60 to buy his very first Walkman before the trip. Two days before the weekend, Omar was pushed and put down by a new boy. Unfortunately he responded with a tirade of his old obscenities and when pushed a second time, kicked the new boy in the stomach and slapped him solidly on the side of the face. All of this took place within view of one of the house parents with the result that Omar's accumulation of 130 points that week was wiped out by 250 penalty points. His Walkman purchase was put on hold and his trip was canceled. He spent that weekend confined to the campus.

The good news was that Omar received some compassionate but firm counseling about his behavior. He learned what caused it and how he could avoid it the next time. It became the topic of his group session a couple of days later. Omar was soon back to accumulating points and privileges. A few weeks later he was finally able to buy his Walkman and thanks to his house parents, who organized a special trip for several guys who had missed the first one, he made it to the zoo. Omar stayed on at the Ranch until he was eighteen. Two years ago, after graduating from a local high school, Omar joined the Air Force, and the last time I spoke to him, he was in training at a military base. After he left, Omar told our treatment team director, "You probably would have assigned points to the air we breathed at the Ranch if you could have. But looking back I can say one thing—the point system was fair, and it's made my adult life easier to deal with."

Counseling

The Lord has blessed His people with time-tested psychotherapies that are an excellent fit within our Christian community. We utilize behavior modification techniques in both day-to-day life in school and the cottages. Individual and group sessions include cognitive behavior modification and reality therapy. Because we're dealing with young people who have specific troublesome issues, the counseling is issue-oriented and answers such questions as: How can each one learn to better trust adults and peers? How can they abate their anger and fear and start to exercise self-control to head off violence? How can they stop thinking about things that keep them depressed and withdrawn? Why do they steal from others and get in so much trouble? Why do they hate anyone in authority and rebel at every turn?

Individual counseling occurs once a week, or more frequently, depending on the need. Crisis counseling is available 24 hours a day. Group sessions are held twice weekly, and whenever possible we include the boy's parent, usually the mother. This is often done twice a month during Sunday visits. Counseling begins as soon as the boy arrives and is usually delivered by his case-worker and perhaps his mother.

People often ask me if the counseling is Christ-centered. My answer is a qualified yes. Therapy sessions employing sound methods generally seek to address modifications of the specific maladaptive behaviors we have discussed. The therapy is basically that which is universally employed by qualified counselors. However, in the sense that the sessions are run by dedicated Christians and that the divine principles such as patience, wisdom, understanding, encouragement, correction, love, and trust are observed, the therapy is more than compatible with our Christian philosophy. During therapy sessions there is not necessarily any Bible-based instruction, although the therapist is free to discuss the spiritual dimension. Chapel services, Bible studies, and youth services off campus are important, but Christ must penetrate each aspect of the program for it to be effective.

Any spiritual issue or question that a child poses during therapy is usually referred directly to me or one of our Ranch chaplains. Counselors are professionals in their field. The chaplains and I are responsible for administering the Word of God and spiritual guidance. Staff members are encouraged, however, to provide a positive witness to the young people and are prepared to encourage them spiritually.

In recent years we've been demonstrably successful in helping 40-60% of the youth who have come here. Considering their moderate to severe emotional and neurological impairment and extreme anger and rebelliousness, this is a phenomenal success rate. I apply the word "success" to any boy who spends 18 months to two years here on a generally upward course of improvement in his personal and social skills, achievement, and work habits. The central question in determining success in severe cases is twofold: Have the young people learned to take care of and regard themselves better than when they came here, and do they relate better to and get along better with others?

Ours is a seemingly gargantuan human task. That is why we rely on Christ for anything we call success. The Bible says that what is impossible with man is possible with God. Some young people have seen their mothers beaten and dragged on the floor; they have heard the most vile, obscene, and violent words shouted at them or others in the home. In some instances, their bones have been broken and their flesh torn. Some have witnessed murder and rape and been sexually abused themselves in the worst ways imaginable.

Desperately needing an adult to look up to, they often are looking into the eyes of a beast. When the adults they look up to abuse them, they conclude in their desperate and confused minds that they themselves are bad; they assume the adult must be good. The young person thinks, "I must be bad, dirty, and worthless." Their psyches, their spiritual cores are invaded, defiled, and damaged, often beyond human healing. The healing of these hurting kids can only come from the One who loved the children and bid them to come unto Him that He might bless them.

Our counseling therapy, education, and spiritual encouragement are aimed at creating a stable structure through which the grace of God, the healing of the Great Physician, and the peace of the Comforter can flow. We at Ranch Hope are just conduits through which the healing can come. We are here to be used and to serve, leaving the outcome to God. I, Dave Bailey, am not in the business of outcomes, only God is. He is the president and chairman of the board of all outcomes. Our goal is to salvage, from the depths of despair, the broken lives of these once innocent and now betrayed victims so that they don't become part of the suicide, homicide, or other statistics mentioned earlier.

An acquaintance I admire, named Ike Keay, puts it

well when he says in his excellent work *Child of Pain, Children of Joy*[24] that these kids are merely on loan to us from God. "For however long these little ones are with us," Ike says, "we and our house parents share with them the good news about Jesus Christ. We teach then God's Word and the principles by which He wants them to live. We try to show them their lives don't have to remain broken, but in Christ they can become the beautiful whole people God intends them to be.

"Because good seed is sown," Ike goes on, "we know these children will never be the same again. Wherever they go, they will know to whom they can turn in trouble or sorrow, They can say with the Psalmist, `When my father and mother forsake me, then the Lord will take me up'" (Ps. 27:10).

For our young people, like Ike's kids at Bethel Bible Village in Chattanooga, Tennessee, the words of the Psalm can become reality. Ours is a place for God to fulfill His promise to take them up after they have been forsaken. It is a place where He heals hurting kids—this is God's neighborhood.

Rev. and Mrs. Bailey with their daughters Lee Ann and Liz and the first boys and staff (1965).

Founder Rev. Dave Bailey surveys furst two buildings (1966)

Early benefactor Hiram Strang receives a picture for "Strang School."

At the dedication of Retzlaff Athletic Center, Congressman Bill Hughes and future New Jersey Governor Jim Florio look on as football great Pete retzlaff speaks.

Rev. Dave Bailey takes a Ranch Hope pig to Howard Katz, owner of the Phil. 76ers. Gen. Mgr. Pat Williams looks on.

Phil. Phillies Phanatic visits Ranch Hope along with NJ Assemblymen Collins and Stuhlrager on the 25th anniversary.

111

Harriet Laury, president of one of our many auxiliaries, at a fundraiser. Completing the picture, Rev. Dave Bailey and two Ranch students.

Reggie White, former all-pro football player, speaks at Ranch Hope banquet and dwarfs Rev. Bailey.

Harry Kalas, voice of the Phillies, receives copy of book Hope for Dead End Kids

The gospel group, "The Hopefuls," raised funds and helped publicize the Ranch ministry.

TV newsman "Mookie" Washington, interviews Ranch Hope student.

Volunteer from local church help with annual Bowl-A-Thon

Children helped each summer at Harvest of Hope, a Ranch ministry to children of migrant workers

Ranch Hope Belgian horses and wagon provide hayride for local visitors

115

Students from Ranch and Victory House cycle to Washington Monument

Jack and Sue Fosbenner with campers at Camp Edge—our new summer program

Dave Bailey, Jr., "Pops" Villegas, and Ranch Hope student appear on ABC's Good Morning, America with Charles Gibson

Ranch Hope and Victory House students visit Hope School in Israel

Ranch Hope Drama Team, called ARMY (Actively Reaching Many Youth) presenting the gospel in music

Director Jim Whitt and his wife Barbara sit with boys and staff at the Home Olympics, an annual event for the boys and girls of Ranch Hope

Chapter 9

Abandoned on Christmas

One of the young people on loan to us from God was someone we'll call Greg, a lanky little kid from Trenton, New Jersey, who had a negative gift for manipulating any adult who came in contact with him. By his own admission he was an artist, a con artist, who had an extremely violent streak. Greg was slick at stealing candy, cigarettes, or anything else that caught his fancy in his neighborhood, seldom getting caught.

At the age of ten he was smoking and drinking and skipping school. At the age of eleven he was smashing furniture in his home and was not beyond trying to break a chair over another kid's head in school. Greg was mean and angry. Often, too often, for him, he managed to smoothly talk his way out of the most outrageous situations and turn the blame on his victim. Greg was growing up to be a big kid, so his violence began to result in greater consequences when an occasional victim wound up in the nurse's office at school or even in the local hospital.

Greg's stealing and truancy ultimately led to his apprehension by the authorities, and by the time he was 12, county agencies had stepped in. By that time, after being confronted by his outrageous behavior and the blame being placed squarely on himself, he took dozens of tranquilizers and sleeping pills, which had been prescribed to him by a doctor. Upon arriving at the hospital, emergency room personnel could hardly believe the enormous amount of drugs Greg had taken, The doctor refused to write in his report the number of pills Greg said he had swallowed the night before, maintaining that if it were true, Greg would not have been conscious to tell about it, he would have been dead. I believe the fact that Greg could not kill himself despite his most extreme efforts is a testimony to the call God had even then on his life. It was a specific and glorious call, but before I get into the details, let's look at what drove Greg to this point of despair and desperation.

When I see Greg now, I see all six feet three inches of him. I also see something that most people don't see, and I praise God for that. I see a boy about four years old living in a dark and cramped trailer with his mom and dad and older brother and sister. To this four-year-old, this was home, a sanctuary where life was reasonably predictable. But was it really?

"My earliest memories," Greg told me, "were of bone-rattling verbal fights and assaults between my mom and dad. The screaming and cursing seemed endless at times in that little box of a home. One Christmas morning when I was playing with my new toys under the Christmas tree, my mother and father were yelling at each other as they often did."

What happened next, Greg recalled, was to shatter the potential joy of all his Christmases to come. "All of a sudden my father was putting on his coat at the door.

"'Where are you going, Daddy?' I asked. 'I'm giving your mother the gift she really wants,' Dad said, and he left. My father did not return minutes or hours later, nor did he ever return. Daddy was gone forever and that thought stuck the terror of abandonment in my heart as a little boy."

Greg's spirit was assaulted and broken, and he became fear-ridden. The person he most trusted had left him alone. At that moment a part of Greg died. *No one can ever be trusted again,* he reasoned. He wondered in the days after Christmas when he would die because it sure felt like he was already dying. He was a defenseless child with a child's mind and fragile emotions trying to interpret what was happening to him. What was truth for him was that he had been left alone to die by his protector and was therefore not worthy to live.

The psychologists tell us that at that time Greg became a fear-based person. In other words, fear totally dominated his mind and emotions. Fear is painful; it hurts. Fear is nasty and unforgiving and is manifested by a top layering of anger, which can be generalized to include all of life—everyone and everything.

Greg prayed like his mother taught him, but one day at the age of seven, his anger turned to the God who was letting him hurt. Because his father had been the first image of God in his life—all powerful, all knowing, and with all wisdom and might over his young life—God became the cause of Greg's pain and the object of his hate. As he knelt in prayer, he cursed God with the most obscene and degrading language. He threatened God and damned Him and told Him he would get even with Him.

Pact With Satan

A couple of years later, Greg saw shows on television about Satan and began praying to Satan for power, the power he felt he did not have. He prayed that Satan would give him supernatural ability to will evil in the world, to kill people with his thoughts, and throw furniture and other objects across the room with an act of his mind.

The relationship that this poor kid had with Satan intensified as the years went on. Greg cursed compulsively. He could not stop cursing, and his speech was laced with the poison of many dark, negative words. The tongue is a powerful creative force that shapes our spiritual life and influences our destiny. The Bible tells us that the tongue has the ability to give life or to put us under. Greg's tongue, as it turned out, put him under.

We tell boys at Ranch Hope that cursing, which to many of them is as naturally as walking, is just what its name implies. When I curse or damn someone or something, I am speaking negatively against God's creation. I am reinforcing a mental attitude and condition of the heart that degrades, demeans, and damns people, places, or things. My view becomes darkened. I am rejecting and condemning that which I have cursed.

As Greg explains it today: "Cursing was like an addiction. It was something that had just been breathed into me. It wasn't something I had to try to do—it was just there. I remember trying consciously to stop it a few times but I couldn't; I had no control over the cursing at all. Sometimes I yelled so long and so loud at God that I couldn't speak anymore from the exhaustion."

Greg finally cursed, stole, and lied his way to Ranch Hope. In the end it was his hatred of school that brought his case before his local school board and caseworkers. This was after he had been before a judge a couple of times.

"When I got to the Ranch, a funny thing happened—I stopped cursing. My house parent would share with me about his horrible childhood, drug addiction, and life on the streets of south Bronx. He was a rough looking guy, and I was sort of intimidated by him. He would just share stuff with me and tell me how Jesus loved me and cared about me. I was impressed that such a rugged guy could be so kind and personally concerned about me. He would take me to church and read the Bible to me. He'd play ball with me. He showed me he cared. I can never adequately explain to anybody the unbelievable feeling of relief I had when I stopped cursing.

"My house parent was the biggest influence behind my becoming a Christian, After about a month of ignoring the altar calls at the chapel, I was convicted in my heart one Sunday and allowed myself to be led up to the altar by some of the guys. I accepted Jesus Christ as my Lord and Savior right then and there, and I began to cry for the first time I could remember. I was amazed that I was feeling something that was true peace. After that I would share with others what God had done for me, that I was no longer at war with life; for example, I would grow more spiritually and emotionally. So I continued to share with the others and see the miracles that He would do for me.

"I was in the Ranch residential treatment program for two years and then went to Hope Home, which is the Ranch's home group house where guys who are making it live like a family and go to the public schools off campus. My house parent at Hope Home was the toughest man I've ever been around, Bill Liebeknecht. He was like a drill sergeant, and every second of our day was structured. I resented it then, but as I look back I really appreciate the difficult and painful times he brought me through. If it wasn't for that man I wouldn't have learned about discipline and order. I grew spiritually from my house parent at the Ranch, but I grew to be a disciplined man with an orderly lifestyle through Liebeknecht. He and God made me a success. Even now when I get up in the morning, I make my bed. When I go away, I fold my clothes and pack them neatly. At work, my work is done on time. I hated that man at times, but there is no one who shaped me as a man like he did."

On to Ministry

That's a pretty remarkable testimony from a kid who recovered miraculously from spinal meningitis, blasphemed God, formed an alliance with the devil, and cursed the world and everyone in it. Even more remarkable is that Greg went on to graduate from high school and college, and became a social worker working with young people for a well-known Christian agency in New York City. Not only that, Greg is now attending seminary out west. He wants to be a minister, social worker, or in some profession where he can serve others.

The thing I recall most about Greg is that he was extremely rebellious when he first arrived here and had a horrible relationship with his mother, a very angry and upsetting woman who really didn't want him to be here. He had some knock-down, drag-out encounters with her. He was not one of the highly aggressive kids who was having a fight every day, but he had a lot of latent hostility to the program. The next thing I knew, Greg had made a commitment to Christ.

We have our share of so-called jail house or foxhole

conversions here at the ranch. A boy will see the house parents and other staff members praising boys who've accepted the Lord and giving them a little extra attention, so he'll make a trip to the altar call, recite the required words, and imitate the buzz words of praise and gratitude that people who have truly accepted the Lord often use. When a person truly accepts Jesus and is filled with the Holy Spirit, there ought to be a demonstrable change of heart that manifests itself in new attitudes and a new language, so to speak. This is found in varying degrees in different people.

Conversion or Con?

Boys who have not had a genuine spiritual conversion but are playacting in order to manipulate the staff have several telltale signs that they are not aware of. We, however, are experienced in detecting them. For one thing, we can usually see the jail house conversion go through a four to six week cycle. That is about all the pretension that any kid can pull off as we give him the benefit of the doubt and take him at his word. We begin to see their regression spiritually as they go back to their old ways of talking and walking. Of course, this regression can also be characteristic of a kid who really had a conversion, but is under spiritual attack and is being sucked back into his old ways.

Our antennae go up when we see this, and we always step in to help both kinds of boys as much as we can. We can minister to the truthful boy and help him not to backslide, but the untruthful kid who never really was converted is not going through the same disappointment. In either case, we don't condemn, but merely help the boy to see how things can be set right.

We had a boy named George, who was Episcopalian in background. He came to my office one day and told me he wanted "to be a Christian." The fact that he had stopped by the office for this was unusual to begin with. So I asked him to sit down, and I explained to him what it meant to give one's life to Jesus Christ. I explained this step by step according to what we call the "Roman road to conversion," that is, what the Book of Romans says on the subject. George prayed along with me, and I led him to Christ. He willingly accepted Him as his Savior.

Six weeks later George earned his first pass home. I subsequently got a call that he had been picked up by the police in Atlantic City for shoplifting. I drove to Atlantic City, about an hour away, got George out of there and took him back to the ranch. On the way back I said, "George, six weeks ago you came to Christ. You've been in Bible study class and everything. Now you get your first pass, and you get busted for shoplifting. How do you explain that?" George's reply spoke volumes about his so-called conversion. He said, "I was convinced that the Lord would protect me from the cops." Well, the Lord does not protect any Christian from stealing or any other obvious sin, and I use George as an example of the antithesis of Greg. I learned to detect the difference. George went from bad to worse after that. He ended up on drugs and in reformatories and penitentiaries. Obviously he had no experience with Christ. He just recently got out of jail after doing a seven-year stretch at a state prison in New Jersey.

With Greg, on the other hand, the presence of Christ in his life was both obvious and genuine. It was a total turn around of his personality. He began getting things together for the first time in his life. He suddenly became a dynamic force on the campus as he witnessed to other boys and became deeply involved in the Scriptures. He was on fire in terms of helping the other kids.

The problem we ran into was that Greg's mother and her paramour, both of whom seemed to have serious problems with alcohol, were opposed to every good thing that happened to Greg after he gave his life to the Lord. His mother's boyfriend would frequently call us here to complain about this or that and to demand that he be sent home to live what they called "a normal life" with them. Naturally the courts and the school board had decided that his home was not what Greg needed, but this did nothing to quell the interference from the boyfriend, who was a pretty mean character and caused a couple of real incidents when he showed up in person at the Ranch.

When Greg attended high school while living here at Hope Home, he developed into a good student and athlete. He was about six feet tall and solidly built. He was very good at basketball and football. It was difficult to believe that this was the same troubled boy who had come to Ranch Hope only a few years before.

I recall a couple of times when Greg's achievements attracted the local newspapers, and they wanted to do a story on him. His mother and her friend threatened to sue us, but the stories appeared anyway. Greg overcame this negative pull from home, although many boys don't. But Greg turned out to be one of the most articulate witnesses for Christ and for Ranch Hope that we've ever had. He is one of the few boys who has returned here to speak to the other kids and encourage them not to quit but to press on. The anointing on his ministry was obvious when, as a 24-year-old social worker, Greg gave a talk to about 700 people in our gym. We could tell then that he was headed for ministry. We assisted Greg with his tuition to a Christian college and helped him scout out a graduate school!

Today Greg is in a nearby city where he ministers to inner-city kids and their families. His word is dedicated to breaking Satan's generational hold on hurting kids who inherit the hurt of their parents and, in turn, hand it down to their own offspring. I see Greg as a rising star in the Lord's galaxy of dedicated workers. He proved to us that our God is not limited in who He can heal or to what extent He can heal. His desire is to make first those who were last.

Chapter 10

From Heroin to Hallelujah!

Ranch Hope has been richly blessed over the years with many memorable people, some of whom we have already introduced to you. Another book would have to be written to tell about all these people, but we've chosen this chapter to profile several whose stories are powerful testimonies about how Christ has moved during our three decades.

In the mid-1970s, Tony Rocco applied for a job at Ranch Hope working with the kids. This was right after he had spent some quality time getting straight at a Christian alcohol and drug rehab a few miles away. I was reluctant in those days to consider job applicants from this center because our experiences with them had not been very good in the past. They just didn't work out. I did not have much experience dealing with adults who had been delivered from alcoholism and drug addiction in those days.

Tony had had a tough childhood in the south Bronx. His earliest memories were of a mother and father who constantly fought. Eventually his violent father abandoned him. Tony got into alcohol when he was just 11 years old and was smoking marijuana and taking other drugs when he was 13, at which time he began being institutionalized. By the time he was 14 he had dropped out of school and had begun shooting heroin. His addiction grew so bad that he left home, and for the remainder of his teen years until the age of 22 he was a street junkie. He lived on roof tops in the Bronx and began dealing drugs to feed his own habit while he ate from garbage cans.

Tony went through numerous juvenile centers and drug rehabs during his teen years. Even though he came to the Lord when he was 15, the constant lure of the streets and drugs saw him relapse regularly and slide away from God.

Prison and drugs were a way of life for Tony until 1972. In 1971 he married Lydia whom he had met while pushing drugs. Tony promised to give up drugs, and they tried to make the marriage work, but Tony soon slipped back into his old ways. It was after their third separation, when he found his way to Mission Teens, a Christ-centered recovery facility for teenagers and young adults a few miles from Ranch Hope. At Mission Teens, Tony was fed a constant diet of the gospel of Jesus Christ. (It is a place where they speak the Word of God day and night.) Eventually he gave his heart completely to the Lord and received the Holy Spirit. Tony was at first turned down on his application at Ranch Hope. But a year later a vision he had for working with troubled boys motivated him to reapply. It was then that I think Tony's spirit and mine began to connect, and we hired him. I also got to know his wife Lydia.

At first I didn't think Tony was happy here or that he was really ready to settle down. During the first few months, I got the impression that he didn't like me, but I didn't know why. Keep in mind that Tony had come from the filthy life in the gutters of the south Bronx. It was very difficult for him to smile or be relaxed. He had very little sense of humor and was basically a pretty uptight person, which was understandable. During those first years, though, Tony was growing consistently in the Word. His wife Lydia was very strong in the faith and became a great stabilizing force in his life.

It was not long before I came to know a different Tony Rocco. I was impressed by his knowledge of the Scriptures and his ability to retain that knowledge. He was a real thinker. He obviously was relating well to the boys and eventually became one of our better house parents. He not only related at their level but was giving them a positive role model because of how God had worked in his life despite where he had come from.

One of the highlights of our relationship was when Tony was called to preach, and I had the opportunity to encourage him to develop along those lines. Tony was ordained at Mission Teens and started street preaching in the nearby city of Salem. He felt he wanted to begin a fellowship for those who were being saved on the streets. I encouraged Tony to use our chapel, and he began holding services and Bible studies.

At that time our director was dead set against Tony's ministry and opposed my support and encouragement. In fact, it was rather tense until that director left the ranch. Tony was Pentecostal and the director did not trust Pentecostals, although our nondenominational philosophy did not prohibit any Christian from joining our staff.

We've always been more interested in a staff person's relationship with Christ and his or her witness of Jesus as Lord of their lives, rather than how they were led to express it in praise and worship. Some Christian brothers and sisters simply love the Lord through prayer and listening to that small quiet voice that the Bible speaks about. Others are moved to dance and sing as David did, to claim the gifts of God's Holy Spirit as the disciples did in Acts, and to worship Him as Psalm 150 prescribes. Often what is more important than the expression of our relationship with Christ is the practical manifestation of His headship in our lives and whether we are seeking to imitate Him.

At any rate, I thank God that I did not give in to that intolerant director. Tony's faith and gift for sharing the

Gospel has truly built up the staff and the boys over the years. Eventually Tony founded a new church in Salem, which is called the Spirit Life Fellowship. The church has grown substantially, and he now ministers to 200 people. He has also established a soup kitchen that feeds 80 or more people each day under his wife Lydia's direction.

Tony has developed such maturity in the Lord that I am honored to have him fill in for me anytime I am away, or whenever he feels led to take the pulpit. We've become real buddies. I also have recommended Tony as a speaker at many churches and youth assemblies because he has become such a powerful preacher. Kids get real quiet and their mouths occasionally drop open as he tells them what his life was like with heroin and what God has done for him.

Tony was with us for 19 years. His sons, Isaac and Tony, were both born while he and Lydia were living here. He not only was our senior house parent but became residential administrator. Tony recalls when house parents put in a 53-hour week here at the ranch before we realized that was too stressful. House parents these days work a 40 or 45-hour week—four days on, four days off—and have the help of night proctors who are on duty after lights out.

Tony Rocco knows better than anyone what it's like to live one's "life in a fishbowl." However, he still talks about the house parenting as being "the most rewarding and gratifying job, because you really get to see up close how a boy grows and changes during a year or two." In speaking with me about what to include in this book, Tony told me that it is a blessing and honor to pray with and encourage these needy boys, seeing them in times of joy and times of great trial. By the way, Tony had a T-shirt made up after his first decade that read: "I survived 10 years as a house parent at Ranch Hope."

"Living in the cottage really was a fish bowl existence," Tony says, "because if I told the kids that they should not be disrupting each other and went into my apartment and disrupted my wife or my children, they would see that. So by virtue of living here I was grateful to be able to demonstrate to these kids a real alternative to what they had experienced so they could see what a real family was.

"You know, my sons first learned to crawl in the lounge with the boys there to watch, and they learned to walk there. The boys and my family had a real family life in the cottage, and they were made part of the family."

Not everything was a Father Knows Best or Donna Reed type existence though. Tony also recalls being awakened in the middle of the night by a boy with his eye cut or by one with a bedpost through his leg. That forces a person to grow.

What amazes me about Tony and other house parents that came from similar drug backgrounds is their excellent stress management. As the secular world is well aware, addicts recovering from years of abuse must learn how to deal with life without their drugs, which had previously served as crutches and helped them to get through life. They must learn a whole new way of living and coping. Those who don't change eventually "go back out" and use again. For most recovering addicts and most of us so-called normal people, being married is stressful enough. Having a child is even more difficult and having two or more is pushing the needle into the red zone. Picture yourself as a former drug addict with a wife and kids. You then voluntarily place yourself in a home with eight emotionally disturbed kids. How do you think you'd handle it? Tony did it not for a year or two, or even for five years, but for ten years without burning out. That's a mighty testimony to God's grace and mercy, and a tribute to the One who is our Great Physician.

Tony says that his key to survival amid such challenges and pressures is his relationship with the Lord Jesus Christ. "When a kid curses you out or threatens you," he says, "Jesus provides the power and discipline and insight to know that the kid isn't angry at you but is reacting from the horrible things in his background. You don't take it personally, you lean on the Lord, you apologize when you make a mistake, and you constantly provide spiritual input to his life. You develop a relationship with him, pray with him, and teach him to pray at night"

House parenting is a phenomenal opportunity to

drop the seed of God into a young person's heart. Boys and girls stand in awe of an adult who takes a personal and patient interest in them. As child psychologists tell us, bedtime is an extremely important time of the day for a child. If bedtime is made a quiet and peaceful time, a youth can be very receptive to the positive input of prayer and guidance.

Tony and other house parents are called to demonstrate God's love by being fair, loving, and firm, all in the name of Jesus. Fruit doesn't always come right away; sometimes it takes a year or two or even three before a boy responds. Some never respond. So a house parent's reward must come not only from the victorious moments when a boy responds and grows before his eyes, but also through his daily labor as one by one he plants those seeds.

In the course of his many years here, Tony witnessed the changes in what we called the emotionally disturbed boy. He has seen how the changes in society and the nuclear family have made the average kid who comes here much more needy than his predecessors. Among other things, there has been a dramatic change in the way our boys react to life, sometimes because of alcohol or drug experimentation. We are also seeing worse neurological impairments due to the mother's drinking while the child is in the womb, which produces fetal alcohol and drug syndrome.

Years ago, Tony would look at a troubled boy and

have faith that he could be helped if he was shown, among other things, how to bring his feelings under control. But the neurological damage is sometimes a very difficult barrier to break through.

As Tony sees it, there is a great need in residential treatment nationwide to provide the type of close, one-on-one relationships and supervision that are available to our boys. Only the love of God can help some of these boys, and only a Christian adult taking them under his or her wing can make the difference in their lives, half of which have been spent in institutions. Tony's brother-in-law, Willie Villegas, who was also a house parent here with his wife Connie, took one of our boys literally under wing—the couple adopted him. That boy was once working at the Ranch under his uncle, Tony Rocco. Is this an amazing story or not? Can you imagine that little 15-year-old drug addict, Tony Rocco, who once slept in alleyways and on rooftops in a heroin-induced stupor and sold drugs to other kids whose lives were messed up, becoming the residential director of Ranch Hope? His department was and is the largest at the ranch. At one time he supervised 52 people. Tony didn't do a good job—he did a great job—and is one of God's walking miracles. Tony is now the chaplain at Ranch Hope and continues to minister at his growing church, Spirit Life Fellowship, in Salem, New Jersey.

Mr. Stu

Charles Studioso, "Mr. Stu" as our boys call him, is

another treasured member of our staff. With his wife, Julie, Charlie administered Hope Home, our residential group home where young people who had graduated from the residential program were permitted to live in a less structured environment. They were allowed to attend public school or vocational school and work off campus. Charlie is also the founder of our weekend coffee house. This is a program where boys and girls outside the Ranch come to socialize and minister with our youth. The evenings include gospel groups, devotions, and refreshments. The coffee house has been responsible for many kids coming to Christ, and this ministry has continued for many years.

Like a number of our other counselors, before coming to Ranch Hope Charlie led a life of crime and addiction which began at an early age, His mother and father separated when he was just six months old. Charlie did not have a father until his mother remarried when he was eleven. He and his stepfather did not get along at all during those difficult years in Brooklyn.

Charlie's career of petty crime and street gangs escalated at about age eighteen. After realizing how nasty and violent he was when he was drinking alcohol, Charlie switched to LSD, cocaine, and just about any other chemical that could ease the pain of the shootings, stabbings, and meaningless lifestyle he was pursuing. After being married for a few years, he started giving his life a second look and saw that it had deteriorated into

139

regular heroin use and selling cocaine. As he was being arrested in his apartment for pushing cocaine, his teary-eyed stepdaughter looked up at the policeman who was handcuffing Charlie and asked plaintively, "Are you going to arrest my Daddy?" Charlie knew then that his life had come to the point where he was actually manufacturing pain—pain that was hurting him and all those around him.

While in jail, Charlie had plenty of opportunity to reflect. He was visited by a young man named Jose, who worked for the Salvation Army's drug program. Charlie was released into one of New York's first Christian rehab's, a place in the Bronx called "Way Out." There he came to know Christ and after four months found himself searching for more of Jesus at Mission Teens in Norma, New Jersey. Charlie was baptized in the Holy Spirit at the Mission, and he came up through the ranks there to be its residential director for one and a half years. With this experience he was invited to join the Ranch Hope staff. Starting as a child care worker in the residential program, he soon had a reputation for loving young people and a genuine concern for their rehabilitation and redemption.

After working at the ranch for a while, Charlie took a leave of absence from his residential staff position and went to Wisconsin to help with Mission Teen's new center. Charlie had been divorced by his first wife; but while there, he met the woman who was chosen for him by God. Julie was a teacher at the Wisconsin mission, and Charlie sensed both her intelligence and the heart she had for helping kids in trouble. After marrying in the summer of 1986, he and Julie headed back to New Jersey with their new family.

Charlie tells me that the joy of his calling comes when he sees the results of what the Lord has done in the individual lives of the boys who leave the ranch and return years later. The former residents often report how they have been blessed emotionally, spiritually, and physically.

Pop Villegas

Thanks to God, the ranch has become a family affair in more ways than one. A great example of this is a guy we call Willie or "Pop" Villegas. The brother of Tony Rocco's wife, Lydia, Willie is now the Residential Division Manager here with a staff of 40 under his care. He came to work here when he was in his 20s after spending a couple of years in the same discipleship program that Tony and Lydia graduated from—Mission Teens in South Jersey.

Willie had been through it all. Born in the Bronx and one of six kids, his parents were divorced when he was just seven. Because his mother worked day and night to support the family, Willie virtually raised himself, if that's what you would call it. He spent his early years on the streets and in harm's way. The result was that by the time he was 13 he was drinking alcohol, at 15 he was heavily involved with marijuana, and at 17 he was hope-lessly hooked on heroin.

As a high school dropout, Willie never worked in the traditional sense. Instead he sold drugs, stole, and ran all sorts of cons to finance his habit. He spent a lot of time in prison, including ten months at Rykers Island in New York when he was twenty-one. At one point, having been released from prison and doing as well as he could in a methadone maintenance program, Willie felt that he needed to get away from New York in order to survive. But he didn't know how to leave or where to go. He heard from his sister, Lydia, that she was doing well at Mission Teens. Although not convinced that the Mission's program was for him, Willie set out for south Jersey anyway. After 26 months at the Mission, Willie moved to Cape May, got his own place, and a job at a clam processing plant. I should quickly add that Willie met a girl named Connie Bridge while he was at the Mission. She is the daughter of a good friend of mine, Reverend Richard Bridge, who was mentioned in an earlier chapter. Willie and Connie soon married, and with the support of his sister and new in-laws, he became the youth leader at Rev. Bridge's church. With that experience behind him, Willie eventually made it onto our staff.

These days Willie will tell you how the Lord miraculously worked in his life to fill in all the gaps that occurred in his upbringing. He never experienced a father-son relationship, for instance, and never learned a work ethnic. He grew up with very low self-esteem. Because of all this, Willie had been a quitter with little confidence in his ability to ever amount to anything and a dim view of the world. But the Word of God told Willie to cast his cares upon the Lord, for He cared for him. Psalms told him that although his mother and father abandoned him, the Lord could lift him up and restore the years that were stolen from him. (Our young people now sing a song with the words, "I went to the enemies camp and took back what he stole from me." What a testimony!) As Jesus began working in his life, Willie says, he learned responsibility—how to show up on time for a job, how to relate to others, and how to be concerned for other people and love as Christ loved.

Pop Villegas still recalls how poorly he used to handle money. No one had ever showed him how to budget and save, or how to manage and balance a checking account. It was his wife, Connie, who at first served as the couple's bookkeeper and helped Willie learn about handling finances. They have been blessed more than they have ever hoped for or imagined. They have three daughters and six grandchildren. They have accumulated a beautiful home off campus and three rental properties in the area. Willie serves as an elder in Tony Rocco's church and is an anointed preacher of God's Word.

The ranch has also provided Willie with what he calls "some exciting times," not the least of which is his son Paul. Paul was originally one of Willie's charges here at the Ranch. Orphaned and with no one he could turn to, Paul one day asked Willie and Connie to adopt him, and of course they agreed. While Willie is in awe of all that God has blessed him with, those who know Willie are in awe of how he has given of himself. In 1991 he was named by state officials as house parent of the year for southern New Jersey.

Jim

Back in the early 1960s when I was trying to figure out how to get Ranch Hope started, Jim Bracken was youth director at the United Methodist Church in Glendora, New Jersey, near what would one day be the Ranch. The pastor was my friend Rev. Richard Bridge. I first met Jim when he was a counselor at a summer camp, and I was the guest speaker. I knew shortly after talking to him that he had a real heart for working with kids. When Eileen and I were struggling to cope with the first group of boys, Jim and his wife Isabel became our first substitute house parents. They relieved us on weekends, serving part-time without pay. These were the days I spoke of earlier when we had the "Dirty Dozen" boys, all of whom were absolute terrors.

In order to explain how Jim and Isabel made it through those days, I must tell you that Jim had known the Lord since he was eight years old. During his 20s he had backslid, as we say, which means he wasn't walking with Christ. He reestablished his relationship with the Lord when he was twenty-eight. Isabel did not know the Lord when they first started working here.

At the time we were having big problems with one of the Dirty Dozen, a boy named Kenny, Jim told me that if I decided to discharge him from the Ranch, that he might consider taking him into his own home, perhaps as a foster child. The day arrived when I told Jim that we were ready to say goodbye to Kenny. Jim phoned his wife to ask how she felt about taking him in, and Isabel said she thought it was okay. But the next day Isabel called Jim and said she was thinking of leaving him, just like that.

The interesting thing was that on his way home to talk Isabel out of her decision to leave him, Jim heard the Lord direct him to first stop by the Ranch. While he was at the ranch, his minister unexpectedly stopped by his house and was ministering to Isabel. To make a long story short, Isabel was saved that very day. Jim still recalls how his wife came to the Lord through a crisis at Ranch Hope. And, of course, she not only did not leave Jim but has been his faithful helpmate for more than 40 years. Kenny lived with Jim and Isabel for a while but turned out to be one of those hard cases. He finally made it into adulthood and is doing reasonable well today in a town north of the Ranch. He was saved from drug addiction at a Salvation army rehab center. Kenny is also active in our Alumni Association of former students.

Looking back, I can now see how the Spirit of God began moving throughout this part of our state in the mid 1960s, seemingly in anticipation of what that godless decade of rebellion would do to young people. The 60s were the years when parents became estranged from their children, started spending less time with them, and became more involved in adultery and divorce. Society began freely embracing all sorts of sinful alternatives to God, and people began leaving their local churches.

In our part of New Jersey, all these things were happening. In addition, however, God was providing havens of healing wherever there was prayer, worship, and obedience to His Word. One of these was a rehab center for African-American kids in Bridgeton and another was to later be established by Jim as a Christian rehab for kids, a vision that began developing while he was at Ranch Hope.

Jim's youth ministry in his church had grown incredibly and became closely linked with his work here. He had large numbers of kids in basketball and baseball leagues and social programs at the church. As he tells it, however, he was not getting through to the kids about the good news of Jesus Christ. They weren't all accepting the Lord.

Frustrated, Jim began asking God to show him what needed to be done to win these troubled kids to Jesus. That's when Jim received the Baptism of the Holy Spirit. In 1965, a revival swept through his church and youth ministry and spread to other churches. Kids were coming to Christ in large numbers, including ten guys from the Ranch. The leaders of Jim's church were not too pleased with the revival, and he and the kids were kicked out. So Jim and Isabel took their ministry to the streets. They started coffee houses and went to places like Camden and to the beaches of Atlantic City and Wildwood in the summer to evangelize young people wherever they found them, This all began two years before during what is now known as the start of the charismatic renewal in our nation. Jim's work continued through the period when drugs began sweeping through suburbia.

In 1969 Jim found an old building in the countryside with 15 bedrooms. He bought it for $24,000 and established Mission Teens, the Bible-based rehab for teenagers. It now takes in people from 18-62 years of age. Most rehab programs will regard a recovering person as a student or a patient, depending on the type of facility. Mission Teens regards its residents as family members, which is why many of the residents go on to become members of the staff. This all comes from being fed the Word of God and worshiping for five and a half hours each day.

Problem addicts and alcoholics were not kicked out of Mission Teens after two or three weeks as they are in secular rehabs. The program is eight months long, after which time some of the graduates stay on for a year of staff training. They are encouraged to stay as long as they feel it is necessary. Mission Teens is the rehab where Tony Rocco and his wife were working before coming to Ranch Hope. In fact, over the years, 26 boys from Mission Teens have served on our staff. Boys who leave here and get in trouble on the streets back home have gone to Mission Teens with miraculous results.

Mission Teens is not for the average addict or alcoholic. Almost all Mission Teens people have previously been to at least two or three rehabs and some up to a dozen with little success. But Jim reports that most Mission Teen graduates who remain for the entire course stay off alcohol and drugs for good—and for God.

Jim's staff is now made up entirely of graduates and all are unpaid. I guess the Lord liked what Jim did with Mission Teens because Jim now has other missions across the world, such as Tuscumbia, Alabama; Fort Lauderdale, Florida; Gaastra, Michigan; Durango, Mexico; and Poland. Our prayers are with him as he and the Lord plan even more missions.

Eddie

A few miles from Ranch Hope on a sprawling 48-acre tract of farmland is a Christian drug rehab for men founded and run by two of our former house parents, Gigi and Eddie Torres. Hundreds of guys addicted to heroin, cocaine, marijuana, and other drugs have been saved by Christ's amazing grace at this place.

Eddie Torres is an amazing guy himself, as we found out when he came to the Ranch many years ago. It was at Ranch Hope that God provided him with an opportunity to learn something about how to run an institution of this kind. Eddie came to New York with his family when he was 12 years old and spoke hardly any English. He went to school but couldn't develop a normal social life because of his inability to communicate. No one seemed to be interested in helping him learn English, (This was long before bilingual education, of course.)

So Eddie became a willing sheep and was led into trouble and danger by the wrong group of guys at school. He seemed to always be getting into trouble, and his frustration led to anger, and the anger to resentment. Using marijuana seemed like a good way of making his world go away for a while. Eddie was 13 when he started hanging out in the streets and doing drugs.

Many of you will be surprised to know that Eddie came from neither a broken home nor a troubled home. His dad had a meager but consistent job; his mother took care of Eddie and the rest of the kids. His home life was not great but certainly nothing unusual for an immigrant family.

By the time he was 15, Eddie was using heroin and started a drug career that saw him alternately in and out of jail and rehabs for the next dozen years. During that time he worked as a butcher and in various grocery stores to help support his habit. Eddie fortunately never got hooked on alcohol, but his life of crime and addiction resulted in his spending half of those 14 years as an addict in reformatories and jails.

At the age of 28 while in a rehab in New York, someone introduced Eddie to Jesus Christ, and he received Him as his Lord and Savior. Things changed a lot for him after that, as he will tell you. For example, after he was saved from heroin by the Lord, he hit the road to give his testimony to other addicts and troubled teens, anywhere they would listen to him. He wound up in Chicago for a while, where he met a cute little girl named Gigi who also loved God, and he married her.

While on a vacation in New Jersey, Eddie picked up a newspaper and saw that Ranch Hope was looking for an assistant house parent. He received a questionnaire from us but was reluctant to fill out the line that asked if he had ever been arrested. Eddie decided to come and see me personally. That was in 1970. The vision Eddie had for establishing a Christian drug rehab began to develop more clearly as he worked with us for the next year and a half. We knew Eddie was somewhat of a risk when we hired him. Only about five to ten percent of heroin addicts ever fully recover and stay drug free. Eddie tells us that the percentage at Faith Farm is almost four times that high, which he attributes solely to the healing power of Jesus Christ. In 1972, a farmer in Quinton Township a few miles from Ranch Hope rented Eddie an acre of land and an old farmhouse situated on it. He began with two heroin addicts and put them through what was the prototype of Faith Farm's 9-month program of recovery. He and Gigi had three children by then.

Today Faith Farm is a licensed drug and alcohol rehab. Its program is structured around a day that begins at 7 a.m. and ends with lights out at 11 p.m. In between these hours, the recovering men have various periods of Bible study, prayer, chores, and classes to qualify them for a high school equivalency diploma. This greatly increases their chances of employment when they leave. A prayer and worship service is held each evening at 7 p.m.

The guys who come to Faith Farm arrive there through referrals from probation departments, clergy, and the courts, as well as through family and friends. Most have been through at least several secular rehabs with little or no success. They have a great opportunity to meet with success at Faith Farm when they finally meet their Lord and Savior. The year Eddie started the Farm, the total rent and expenses were $4,000. Ten years later he owned the farmhouse and the entire 48 acres. Today Faith Farm has six buildings and maintains a staff of 25 full-time and four part-time professionals, assistants, and other staff. Its daily enrollment is 37 men. Eddie went home to be with the Lord a few years ago, and his wife Gigi has carried on the ever expanding work.

Eddie, Tony, Jim, Charley, and Pops are testimonies to the proverbial truth that God makes mighty men from those who are weak, and that He wishes to use once dead-end kids as witnesses of His glory and power.

Chapter 11

Born Again Tough Guys

Rashon was born and raised on the streets of Newark, New Jersey. As a baby he was abandoned by his mother and father and was brought up by his grandparents, who did their best, but their home was without the Christian faith.

Not surprisingly, Rashon had a lot of problems growing up. By the time he approached adolescence, he was rebelling against everyone and everything. After a couple of years of constant fighting with other kids, truancy at school, and hostility toward his teachers and others in authority, he was placed in a child treatment center about 50 miles south of Newark. While visiting this treatment center, John Dickenson, our director of social services, showed Hassan a brochure about Ranch Hope. John asked him if he thought he would like to go to the Ranch, and he instantaneously agreed, which Hassan now says was God's will.

Rashon is a good example of how we patiently apply the gospel of Jesus Christ. At first he went to chapel reluctantly and did not exactly embrace a Christian lifestyle. He was not a big troublemaker, though he was still a little rebellious. Like so many other boys, Hassan was extremely insecure, scared, and untrusting. During his first two years, he gradually warmed up to some of our staff, but we could tell that he was still inwardly rebellious, angry, and unhappy.

Recalling for me a particular day when he was chiding Tony Rocco for being a preacher, Rashon said, "It reached the point where I at least started to see the love of Christ. Tony made a comment about my spiritual condition, I guess, and I replied with something like, 'Yeah, well you can't preach, either.'"

Instead of responding defensively, Rashon told me, "Tony ministered to me, telling me how much the Lord loved me and about the power available to those who are willing to receive His grace. Meanwhile, I saw that the program here was designed to progressively give guys like me a degree of freedom and not to close them in and make them feel imprisoned."

Rashon also recalled living with his grandparents and longing to have a big brother to play with and look up to. That's partly why he took so well to the Ranch. Here he had lots of big brothers to choose from, and everybody was a brother or sister in the Lord. He felt embraced here and that comforted him and made him feel positive about himself.

The day finally came when Rashon accepted Christ as Lord in his life. In a rather simple moment in our cafetorium, he knelt with one of the house parents and said the sinner's prayer. He describes it today as being set free, "Like I had been all bound up in chains inside all my life, and the Lord broke those chains. I felt light, like I could float. It was a totally different feeling than I ever had before, and I became completely different after that."

Afterwards, Rashon's grandmother couldn't understand why he was more mellow and mannerly each time he returned home to visit. "What on earth have they been teaching you at that place?" she wondered. Even his friends marveled about the change.

Sports, Rashon now says, was one of the things that helped instill a sense of discipline, organization, and co-operation within him. He's one of those boys who makes me proud to have been a notorious sports fanatic all these years (Phillies, Eagles, '76ers, Flyers—a real Philly fanatic).

We would like to accommodate more boys like Rashon, who benefited greatly from Hope Home, our "real house" at the edge of the campus where about ten young people live with house parents and are given rules to live by but also much freedom. Hassan attended the local Woodstown High School and played varsity football. He was also a champion heavyweight wrestler. He was an excellent role model for the students at Hope Home.

Hope Home made it possible for Rashon to stay here for a total of six years, until he was nineteen. We're proud of the growth and maturity he's achieved. On top of everything else, he also became our campus poet and has had some of his work published in our newspaper *The RH Factor*, and the high school paper *The Woodstonian*.

What's next for this kid? Well, Rashon pursued a major in early childhood education and worked with kids after he graduated from Liberty University. He is now in Probation work. Among the boys who accept the Lord and do well here, there is usually implanted within them a burning desire to give back some of what they received. When you know you are loved by God, it is easier to love Him and to love your neighbor. As with all our graduates, he has had his ups and downs—we continue to pray for him. He is often in touch.

Harry

"Dave," the staff caseworker pleaded, "Harry's been turned down by 12 institutions around the state, and we really don't have any other recourse except Ranch Hope. Why don't you give the kid a try?"

We took Harry because no one else would. He was 15 years old, over six feet tall, and weighed about 190 pounds. Harry was from a horrendous home where no one, including his brothers and sisters, wanted anything to do with him. This resulted in his being very antisocial and aggressive. He was a brawler, and a brawler only gets respect when he wins the fight. Nice people keep their distance from people who fight as a way of life. This made Harry a big, and very lonely kid.

Harry's behavior did not impress the boys with whom he was now sharing a cottage, though. They were totally unsympathetic. One day I came running down to his cottage on an emergency call. Harry had received a dose of his own medicine—the worst broken nose I think I've ever seen. It was splattered all over, courtesy of our Ranch Hope boys who felt that Harry needed an attitude adjustment delivered to his face. After the nose healed a few weeks later, the boys decided Harry's attitude had not healed. They began brutalizing him in the middle of the night as he lay asleep in his bed. His transgressions of the day were paid back in the evening. They attacked him and punched him silly while he was sleeping.

Harry would go to sleep weeping, but because he was so badly bruised, joy did not come in the morning. It didn't take too much of this before his behavior finally began to change. He was startled that anyone could do him in. We were concerned at one point that these kids might seriously injure Harry one day. We were about to do something about it when his attitude suddenly did adjust. What made it really hard on Harry was that while we were trying to minister to him and help him, he never had any family visits. No one came to see him or even called him. We were working in a vacuum, or so it seemed. As I said, Harry was a big, lonely kid.

His life really started taking a change for the better when David and Faith, a couple of youthful house parents, took Harry under their wing. They began witnessing to him and taking him off the campus to the Christian coffee houses that were popular with "Jesus people" in the early 1970s. Harry took a liking to all this, especially the personal attention.

In no time at all Harry became enthusiastically wrapped up in all the Christian rallies and meetings and gave his life to the Lord at one of the coffee house gatherings. What happened after that was another of the miracles we've seen over the years. Harry turned into a completely different person. It was as though a new boy took his place at the ranch. He stopped his hostile acting out altogether. He even became a positive influence on the campus for bringing other kids to Christ. He would invite them to rallies and witness to them about how God had given him a new heart. He was on fire.

Harry had an average I.Q. but was a low achiever academically. That began to change, too. His grades improved and became commensurate with his God-given ability. Harry also had a speech impediment that exacerbated his antisocial problems. The kids would tease him about it, which made him feel bad. After he started walking with God, however, he became amenable to the speech therapy that was available to him at the ranch. The impediment was soon no longer a factor, thanks to the Great Physician.

Harry won our highest award of achievement, the Cowan Award, which is named after John Cowan, an early benefactor of the ranch. Mr. Cowan was a man of great faith, perseverance, and generosity. The boy who once had no honor among his family or peers ended up graduating from our program when he was nineteen. He is one of only a few dozen boys ever to have been elevated to honor ranch hand.

If someone asked me who among our graduates has proven to be the strongest Christian family witness, I would have to answer Harry. He now has his own business, is married to a lovely woman, and the proud father of four children. He has always been employed and is a hard worker. He bought his own handyman's special of a house and fixed it up beautifully. Now in his early 40s, Harry is a blessing to us because we can see how the Ranch is working through another generation. In fact, Harry has been a continuing blessing through the contributions of time and energy to the Ranch.

Harry grew up in other ways, too, He's still big, but he's not lonely anymore. And his nose turned out fine.

Successes or Failures?

A newspaper reporter once asked for an interview. His local paper was preparing a special article on Ranch Hope for their Father's Day issue. As the reporter began to question me about the history of the ranch, I found myself reliving some past experiences I hadn't thought about in a long while. Some of those experiences were fun to relive while others brought back heartaches.

I thought of the hundreds of boys and girls we had helped here at the ranch, but I also had to retell some horror stories of those with whom we had failed. In fact, I shared with the reporter that just moments before he entered my office, I had received a collect call from a Florida jail. The young man calling had been at the Ranch six years before and was seriously troubled. On Christmas we had sent him home for a break, and his drunken father had beat him up on Christmas Eve and sent him back. Is it any wonder the troubled boy is now a troubled man?

The reporter asked me if this type of experience was discouraging. My response was an immediate, emphatic yes! But I quoted an old saying that still makes sense: "I was called to be faithful, not successful." Success is always in the eye of the beholder. We were able to help the young man in prison during some very difficult days in his life. Our staff became the "father" he never had, our school provided him with education he may have otherwise never received, and we continue to be the family for which he cries. Interestingly enough, I was able to contact a Christian pastor in the Florida area, and he visited our young man. In the last phone call I received, the young man told me he was awaiting trial. But he also said he had become involved in Bible study and will use his jail sentence as time to renew his commitment to Christ. You see, while he was with us he was growing spiritually. We planted many seeds in that young life that are only now beginning to grow.

Some of our graduates are like Jonah—they try to run away from the grace of God. The "whale" that consumes them can come in many forms. I pray for the successes and for those with whom we were not very successful. They are all our boys and girls and are still part of our family.

Chapter 12

School and Sports

Ours was one of the first special schools in New Jersey for emotionally disturbed children. It dates back to 1969, the Ranch's third year. Our current academic building, the Strang School and Counseling Center, was built in 1982 next to the Pete Retzlaff Gym. Both are modern buildings and, because of their size, are the dominant features of the campus. School was originally held in a cinder block building that has now been converted into Hunt Lodge, the cottage for boys who have progressed to star ranch hand. In the beginning it was a no-frills schoolhouse.

We are one of the founding members of the New Jersey Association for Schools and Agencies for the Handicapped, an organization which has allowed us to keep our fingers on the pulse of special education. The

Strang School also is a member of the National Association of Private Schools for Exceptional Children and are awaiting approval by Middle States Accreditation. We have made many fine friendships through that network.

For readers with little knowledge of emotionally disturbed and neurologically impaired kids, I need to point out that any school that specializes in working with these children is not like your every day school. As our principal will tell you, however, a major part of our job is to prepare young people for life in the real world. We try to strike a delicate balance between coddling them in an institutional atmosphere and treating them the same as nonemotionally impaired children would be treated in a regular public school. In other words, we try to meet their special needs while at the same time providing as "normal" a school atmosphere as possible.

Some youth return after 18 months or so to the special classes or regular classes of local public schools. They often need special preparation for that. They are not ours for keeps; they are just on loan. The worst thing we could do is make them "institutionalized," meaning allow them to become totally dependent on a special program that doesn't really prepare them for life outside the Ranch.

The Old School

During our planning back in 1964, we decided we

would do our schooling in the lounge of the residential cottage. The boys could sleep in their rooms, eat in the dining room, and under the same roof we would have a school.

What we forgot to plan for was who was going to teach them and what materials we would use. Someone had given us 40 or 50 school books, but unfortunately they were extremely outdated. When we began with our first two students, we dug out these books, which dated back to the mid 1950s, and I was the teacher similar to today's home schooling set-up.

My teaching career was short-lived, however. Inadequate education, poor materials, and lack of space all led to an inadequate school. Two teachers whose husbands we knew—one a minister's wife and the other a prominent business man's wife—came to the ranch and volunteered their help. Mary Woodruff and Billie Ackley were like angels sent from God. Day after day through the whole summer they came to teach the boys for three hours each day.

Perhaps the most unique and humorous technique ever tested for discipline came from a volunteer teacher, a widow in her 60s, who one day decided to fight fire with fire. Because she was such a poor disciplinarian, her class was out of control just about every day. She decided to change this by coming to class in jeans and a sweatshirt. When the students began to act up, she took off her sweatshirt to reveal a tank top shirt with a big karate symbol on it. She boasted that she was a black belt and would demonstrate her ability to incapacitate anyone with one blow of her hand if they did not settle down. Her experiment backfired, however, because all dozen of her boys became terrified and rushed to my office seeking protection. Fortunately the woman returned to her previous employment, and we sought out a less provocative and better trained staffer. Interestingly enough, she later received her degree in teaching and was able to help other youth.

By the time we had a dozen students, the need was increasing for us to have better school facilities. It was difficult for the teachers to teach effectively in a room only 20 feet from the students' bedrooms, right in the middle of the lounge where all the traffic from the ranch flowed through. Our apartment was in the same building with the boys, and our children were only babies then. They had needs, too, and they were making it difficult for the boys to concentrate. These poor women doing the teaching were working under extremely difficult circumstances.

We knew that a real school had to be built, right on campus with good teachers and good materials—all geared toward preparing the young people for high school. In September after the arrival of our first group, we broke ground for the new school building. We only had $450 in the bank, but we knew we had to get started on it. We also needed a shop area for the boys to learn woodcraft and work on their hobbies. All this was to come in due time. We had to take another leap of faith.

Again, the Terrell Foundation was the answer to our prayer with a $25,000 grant to start the school construction.

Intensive Care School

Today, our on-campus Strang School is licensed to accommodate up to 99 students. In past years we have operated just shy of that number. About 60 Ranch Hope residents are taught and cared for by a staff of 11 teachers, 11 assistants and 3 administrators, including the principal. We also have day students who come in with special education needs from other communities. There are eight periods from 9 a.m. to 3 p.m., and the curriculum consists of math, language, arts, general science and biology, computer skills, shops (these include woodworking, auto, and our food service shop at the cafeteria), and everybody's favorite, gym. We duplicate as closely as possible the full spectrum of special education programs. Ours are self-contained classes. Each boy is assigned to a group which moves from class to class to maintain order and discipline.

Until a full time principal came on board, our only classes were elementary level. Soon after he took over, he and other staffers began noticing that some of the older boys were skipping school. They would get bored and take off to fool around in the woods or run around campus, playing hide and seek with the staff. One day the principal caught a few of them who had skipped out and were hanging around one of they picnic tables near the school. More curious than angry, he began questioning them about their reasons for being truant. They complained that they felt like Strang School was set up like a "baby school," and they expressed their wish to be "treated like regular high school kids."

Our principal told the boys that if the school treated them more like high school kids with different subjects and schedules, it would be a lot tougher on them each day. Their response was that they wouldn't mind more challenging classes and schedules, so he began thinking about how to eliminate the scholastic boredom and meet the needs of these boys.

After some discussion with me and the other staffers, the principal recommended that we institute transitional classes for the students who were up to or near high school level. These classes were successful at helping the boys make a smoother transition from elementary to middle school. They were also better prepared for school outside Ranch Hope. If nothing else, these classes were challenging enough to take away the time and inclination they had to retreat to the picnic table or the woods when they should be in school.

Summer School

Strang School conducts a summer school program. It is an expanded academic program that assists students with learning difficulties to improve their skills through small group instruction and one-on-one tutoring.

In addition to the regular academic schedule, students participate in physical fitness activities, swimming, horsemanship, and wood shop. A series of weekly field trips rounds out the program. The students are enthusiastic. One student said that it's good to work on reading during the summer because he needs a lot of help from "when I didn't pay attention in regular school. The swimming and horseback riding are good too." A talented group of teachers and assistants staff the summer program. Regular school staff are joined by an experienced summer school staff.

Exercise is necessary for everyone's mental and spiritual health. We believe our fitness program helps all the boys feel better during their treatment here. There is much for them to learn in organized sports in terms of fairness, competitiveness, and being a good winner and a good loser. Aside from the fact that I have been affectionately called a sports fanatic by some of the graduates, our gym and athletic programs are meant to help each boy to enjoy himself and to better prepare for the pace and competition of today's society.

Ranch Hope is part of a six-school basketball league. We play residential schools and other institutions. The league provides extracurricular activity for the participants and helps develop a real team spirit among everyone here. We have both varsity and junior varsity teams competing.

The boys do well in the tournaments we enter. For example, not one but seven of our talented boys made the state finals of the New Jersey Tournament of Champions track and field meet, which is held at McGuire Air Force Base, about 90 minutes north of us. The team brought home ten medals in seven events, and most of them couldn't have been prouder. What a good memory for healing their self-esteem! During a recent spring, 14 of our boys between the ages of 12 and 15 traveled to Easton, Pennsylvania, to participate in the first National H'Olympics (Children's Home Olympics). They joined with more than 100 boys from homes in Missouri, Pennsylvania, Arizona, Virginia, and Maine. They competed in basketball, softball, swimming, billiards, and track and field. The participating homes are all members of the National Fellowship of Child Care Executives, a professional group of leaders from 68 homes. This event was an excellent time of fellowship, and the boys were able to meet and identify with many other guys who are just like them. This experience helped them all feel better about themselves.

We did our utmost to make the Olympics the really big deal we thought it should be. H'Opening ceremonies were preceded by a parade of athletes just like in the real Olympics. Can you imagine a boy from the inner city, who never played organized sports to begin with, finding himself in a parade of athletes? It was a thrill for the boys and for us. The marchers dressed in brightly colored uniforms representing their home colors. This event occurs each year in different parts of our nation.

There was also a demonstration by world-class athletes from the Scottish Games, which most of the boys had never seen or heard of, with big burly guys from the Scottish highlands throwing things that look like telephone poles. It was wild. Then the kids passed the H'Olympics torch and lit the official flame.

Following the ceremony and the track and field events, and the basketball tournament was held in a double elimination format. One of the things this demonstrates to our troubled boys is that the world can indeed be an orderly, structured place with people close to them who care.

Sports banquets and tournaments are more in the area of fundraising, but we've been blessed to have the sports stars who participate in them also speak to the boys. For instance, we recently had former baseball star Bill Robinson speak at our annual sports banquet. He played for the Phillies, Pirates, and Mets and is always a great inspiration. Mike Schmidt, former all-star third baseman for the Phillies has also visited, as has Reggie White, formerly of the Philadelphia Eagles, and Pat Williams, president of the Orlando Magic basketball team.

Every year, we have our annual Ranch Hope Golf Classic at a nearby country club with former all-pro tight end and general manager of the National Football League's Philadelphia Eagles, Pete Retzlaff. Pete usually invites other sports greats to be with us, and each foursome gets to play with a celebrity The Golf Classic is one of our best fundraisers, and we've made many good friends on this special day. In the 1960s and 1970s, even school sports became a thing of disdain among many young people. The term *jock* sprung up as a derogatory epithet, as though non-participation was somehow more honorable than pursuing athletic prowess.

One good thing that did emerge from that period of reexamination was that winning solely for the sake of winning was not to be idolized and blown out of proportion. Sports for the sake of fitness and competitive sports properly taught and organized make a great contribution to young people everywhere.

Chapter 13

Losers, Winners, and Angels

After 40 years, you can see that we have been blessed with many people and many stories—both sad ones and glad ones. I couldn't possibly tell you about all of them here; however, I want you to know about a few more of the folks, organizations, and events that have made the Ranch what it is. This chapter is a sort of potpourri. You'll notice that we've run into some losers in our time. There have been more winners and angels, however, and I think you'll be able to tell them apart in the vignettes that follow.

Oh, Wilbur!

Dutton, Virginia, is situated in the boondocks about 60 miles north of Norfolk. Without any letter of introduction or even a phone call, a preacher from Dutton drove north to Jersey one day and dropped in to see me. He wanted to start a boys ranch near Dutton. I intended to spend only an hour with him, but the hour soon turned into two and then three and then three and a half. During that time, Wilbur meticulously picked my brain and the brains of several others. We had to summon all our patience, knowing that he was a Christian gentlemen who seemed to want to do God's work.

Two months later I got a thank you letter from Wilbur on the new stationary of the ranch he had founded in Virginia—Hopesville. A few weeks later, he called me from Wilmington, Delaware, with eight other men, his board of directors who were about to open the doors of Hopesville and wanted some more free advice from us. They spent all afternoon here and not only stayed for dinner but did not start heading back to Virginia until 9 p.m. That's not the end of the story.

One afternoon sometime later ,the phone rang in my office and my secretary said it was Wilbur. I said to myself, "Uh, oh, I better prepare for another surprise visit and probably another meal for a dozen guys." Wilbur surprised me in a different way that day, however. He said that he had just received a call from a place in Valley Forge, Pennsylvania, a foundation that had some money it wanted to give away, but neither Wilbur nor Hopesville was eligible.

"We don't qualify and I was wondering if you needed

it," said Wilbur in his down-home, matter-of-fact way of conversing. I tried to be cool and suppressed my wild enthusiasm, so I calmly thanked Wilbur and called the number in Pennsylvania right away. I couldn't even get the name of the foundation because they had a rule that they operated only in anonymity. They asked me to write a letter asking for the sum we needed. At the time we needed $85,000 to finish the Pete Retzlaff Athletic Center, to which the former Eagles football star had already donated his good name.

Although I was hoping we might get $25,000 from this foundation if God really blessed us, I asked for the full $85,000 anyway. I waited. One sunny afternoon I received a direct call from the Foundation, and a gentleman told us that we would receive a grant. I almost fell off my chair when he told me it was for the full $85,000. The athletic center would be built, praise God! Paul says in the Bible that you never know when you might be entertaining angels unawares, That's right, I said to myself back then, you never know when someone may drop in on you from Dutton, Virginia. Don't turn them away; they may be there to drop $85,000 in your lap. Thank you, Jesus!

A Big Help

We wrote a friend who had been wise in financial dealings and had a reputation for good counsel. We knew that he might be able to help us by making a personal contribution or personal loan, or might be able to send us to someone who could help. We wrote a two-page letter describing in detail how desperately we needed someone to pick up the large second mortgage. This letter was sent with a great deal of prayer and hope that we would have some answer to our dilemma. For seven long days we waited for a response. Finally a letter came back. There was no mention of the $8,000 we needed; no mention of where we might borrow it; no mention of any idea that would encourage us. But there was a check enclosed for $10. It was a big help, let's say a widow's mite.

Hiram Strang

One Sunday morning in the early 1960s, there was a tremendous snowstorm with an accumulation of at least two feet in many areas. My wife and I noticed a large milk truck stuck in a snowbank across from the church I was pastoring. We rushed out to see if we could help and found that it was Hiram Strang, a dairy farmer whose wife had been active in our church. We helped dig out his truck, and a friendship developed which was to play an important role in the founding of Ranch Hope. From that initial meeting when we dug snow together, this man's spiritual interests began to be revitalized.

The next summer we had a series of evangelistic services in, of all places, a tent. They were very successful, considering that such preaching services were almost unheard of in that area. Hiram played a major role helping us prepare for them and did much of the labor in setting up the tent. He even helped during the services by collecting money, ushering, and other incidentals. Hiram was deeply involved in running his own farm plus he hauled milk for others. We had no idea the extent of his financial capabilities, and he was the last man we would have thought of in regard to taking a second mortgage on our property. He continues to be one of Ranch Hope's dearest friends—a faithful angel.

Fund-Raising

In the early days, we sat one evening in a restaurant waiting for a locally prominent gentleman to talk with us about our proposed youth home. He was the type of man who did good for the sake of doing good rather than for the sake of praise. For instance, when our bills for seminary and raising a family were not getting paid, it was this man who wrote out a check to get us through the rough spots. Later, he decided to give us $500 to help develop a nest egg to purchase any property we came across to start the ranch. It was at his suggestion that we had a large public meeting to make the Ranch Hope project known to leaders all over our state. It was a banquet, and I had to plan it.

First, I needed to arrange for an outstanding keynote speaker who would draw a good crowd. There were several men I believed could successfully encourage an audience to give to Ranch Hope while not losing sight of our spiritual challenge. We contacted one man who did work much like ours in a large metropolitan area. Much to our consternation, we found that he was not interested at all in accepting any such speaking engagements. Knowing we were not yet operative, I could not understand what we had done to alienate ourselves from a man who was already well-known in the field of social work and Christian preaching.

Still in need of a speaker, we swallowed hard and tried again. This time we tried to reach an equally successful man in our field who we thought could effectively straddle the disciplines of social work and Christian rehabilitation. To our surprise, this prominent individual replied that he would not speak in our area about our work because he needed our area too much as a financial resource for his own work. Not only did this destroy my personal impression of this man, but it made me wonder about nominal Christians. We prayed about that.

Finally we turned to the field of education and a professor who we thought might be successful by taking the academic approach. He agreed to speak but when the evening for our fundraiser finally arrived, the turkey that was the main course tasted excellent to everyone but me. More than 300 people were there, and as we sat down after the invocation, it seemed that Ranch Hope was to be blessed. But half way through the meal, our speaker had still not arrived. I have often wished since then that he had never arrived. As most of our guests were completing the dessert, I was out in front of the meeting place doing more pacing than I had over the births of our three children combined. Finally the professor arrived. After allowing him time to eat a hurried meal, we retired to the sanctuary to listen to him speak.

To say that his talk was disappointing would be kind. It was disastrous. He approached the subject strictly from an academic point of view and did little to inspire his audience to support Ranch Hope in particular or to help delinquent children in general. The tenor of the evening can be sensed in what one ardent supporter said, "If I had had a thousand dollars to contribute to this project tonight, it would have remained in my wallet." Thankfully, this was not the consensus of the audience. In spite of the problem of a rather boring evening, there was a great deal of interest generated among the contingent of probation officers, lawyers, judges, professional people, and ordinary citizens, many of whom were to become the backbone of Ranch Hope.

But let me conclude this part of our story with a "Whoops! You almost had it" story. At the meeting that night was a man very interesting in helping. Tragically he died soon after this while undergoing heart by-pass surgery. As I was visiting with his wife, she told me how much he had loved the Ranch and had wanted to leave a substantial part of his estate to us. My ears perked up. Unfortunately, she told me, he had originally set aside a large sum of money in his will to go to Boys Town some years before and had never changed it to read Ranch

Hope. I thought I was going to have my own funeral that day. Oh well! Talk about the Lord teaching us patience—this was a classic beginning.

John

While looking for a printer to compose and produce our all-important promotional brochure, the hand of God moved again to open doors that had appeared to be very definitely closed. A friend later told us that God may not always open a door, but He will usually at least raise a window, and at this point we believe He had raised one.

I was doing some part-time radio announcing at a local radio station while serving as pastor in Bridgeton, New Jersey. Week after week I read an advertisement over the air about a printer named Cowan. We had recently moved to this smaller church in Bridgeton so we would have more time for developing the ranch. The merchants of Bridgetown were mostly strangers to us, and we had no idea who John Cowan was.

After we had completed a rough draft of the brochure, his name came to mind, I suppose because I had used it so many times on the radio. The question was, would this printer be sympathetic to our needs and how expensive would he be? One weekday we found time to visit his plant. I had made no appointment and therefore wasn't even sure John Cowan would see me.

His plant was very impressive by its outward appearance and gave the impression of being successful.

Mr. Cowan was in his office. His secretary asked me to wait, and after what seemed mere moments, I was face to face with a man who was to become one of the closest friends of Ranch Hope. John Cowan was standing on crutches. He was a tall, imposing man whose face and stance seemed to communicate a busy executive with lots on his mind. He listened quite intently as I described what we wanted to do for troubled boys. He seemed impressed. He took the material we had put together and told us to stop by in a short while, and he would give us a rough draft of what he wanted to do.

After leaving his office we learned a great deal about this man. We had noticed a number of awards hung inconspicuously in the office, and we had sensed an interest in various civic clubs, especially the Boy Scouts. We wondered what had necessitated the crutches. Through mutual friends, I discovered that this man, who was so willing to do so much for others, had been unable to walk for over 20 years. There are people God moves into our lives to inspire us, people who make us feel as though any problem we have is minute. Such people stand as testimonies without speaking a word. They witness without ever entering a pulpit. John Cowan had been given the choice of standing or sitting for the rest of his life because of a serious arthritic condition. John did our first brochure and contributed numerous printing jobs after that, in addition to other generous contributions. He is always in our hearts here at the ranch. After his passing, we named our first cottage "Cowan Cottage" in his memory.

I often look back at that first booklet and laugh when I think of some of the great plans we have since had to alter or even forget. One picture in particular of the old barn. The caption beneath it read, "This old barn will be later used for winter sports, such as basketball and indoor volleyball." It was eventually knocked down, and we built the chapel there.

Best Laid Plans

The plans for the first home were drawn up by a young architect from Pitman named Leroy Davis. Leroy spent a lot of time not only on the blueprints but on the list of specifications. Since his time was donated, he was too busy with paying work to visit the ranch to inspect the construction as often as he would have liked.

Knowing that a mason had been working on a building for three weeks, Leroy stopped by one afternoon to check the progress. I was not prepared for what he discovered.

"Dave, Dave, what's happened to this building? Who's messed up my plans? I can't believe this; I can't believe what I'm looking at." He was almost screaming as he rushed from wall to wall

"What's the problem, Leroy?" I asked, trying to seem calm. "Everything looks fine to me. Those guys have really laid some block in less than a month. I think the work is fantastic, don't you?"

"I think it is a disaster!" Leroy interrupted. "Where is that mason? Look at these walls, Dave; they are out of plumb. Look at the mortar between the block; it is all uneven. Stand back and eye up that doorway; it's uneven. A door will never fit in there."

Leroy was close to a major nervous breakdown, and as he pointed out mistake after mistake, I was ready to join him.

"David," Leroy said, "fire those guys; get them off the Ranch. All their work will have to be torn down and we'll start over again. Go tell them what a mess they've made." And so we did, and Leroy, not one to be discouraged, stayed on with us and was a great help with several more buildings.

Concrete Faith

Herb Fithian from Owens-Illinois in Bridgeton had lined up 30 men to meet at the Ranch one Saturday morning. They were going to finish the job on our first cottage, Cowan Cottage, in one big herculean effort. The first truckload of concrete was ordered for 6 a.m. with other loads ordered to arrive every 45 minutes there-

181

after. By 7:30 a.m. I had three truckloads of concrete (seven cubic yards in each truck) sitting, churning round and round, but no men.

The drivers were very impatient "Where's your help, Reverend?" one of them asked as he jumped down to add some water to the mixer. I overheard another one not so graciously say to his buddy, "There ain't nobody gonna show; let's drop this stuff and go home."

I was convinced the Lord would bring the help, but I had a tough time persuading three burly truck drivers of His faithfulness. Each of them had visions of the concrete setting up before any of it was poured. Suddenly down the road came six cars, each one packed with men. They arrived not one minute too soon, and Herb Fithian jumped out making apologies. "These guys had to have some early morning coffee and buns, and a couple of them had a hard time getting started on their day off."

I couldn't have cared less that they were late; I was just praising the Lord that they had made it at all. Herb immediately took charge and barked the commands, "Okay, you guys line up here; get these wheelbarrows and let's start unloading this concrete." Unload they did. By late that Saturday afternoon, all of us had pitched in and all but two rooms were poured and finished off. It was just another reminder that the Lord would raise up workers for His ministry even before we took the first boy.

Chris

One of the most frustrating six months of my life was before Chris, whom I mentioned earlier, was sent off to a reformatory. The church I was working for at the time had a large congregation, its Sunday school drawing 300 people each week. Chris would faithfully come, but never quite fit in. We counseled him for an hour on Sunday morning, but he always felt a little out of place. This church was on a higher social and economic level, and he and his family were like the proverbial fish out of water.

We quickly realized that one hour a week of contact was insufficient to really help Chris. We visited his home on many afternoons. Each time, he would introduce us to another "relative," usually a man. I had only been out of seminary a short time and was still idealistic about human nature. We believed that those guys were really relatives. Later on, of course, we discovered that each man was a paramour of the boy's mother.

Chris' father had once had a lucrative job in an industry not far from his home, but had become addicted to alcohol. One weekend he abandoned the mother with her seven children, From then on the family deteriorated. Is it any wonder, I thought, that this boy is having problems? He was a classic example of a delinquent with an unconcerned father leaving the family and a mother , unable to control her family becoming involved with other male companions, all the while giving her children more and more excuses for misbehavior. The question

183

that plagued me was what would be best for this boy. Because of the frustration of dealing with Chris, we were finally driven to our knees in seeking God's answer, which became Ranch Hope. I thank God for him.

A Thousand Moms

Mrs. Eleanore Meyers called us one day to inquire how she could help with the Ranch. We had a number of phone calls like that from people wanting to know how they could help, but few ever materialized into anything productive. They were simply kind gestures. We thought Mrs. Meyers was just another one of these well-intentioned callers, but thankfully, we were wrong.

One afternoon she invited a few of her friends over to her home to hear me speak to them about our vision for Ranch Hope. At this first meeting we started the auxiliary. These first four women soon multiplied into hundreds of dedicated workers who raise funds, gather clothing, get out publicity, and gather goods and household products for Ranch Hope. Within a year that one auxiliary had expanded into three. Within three years, those auxiliaries had expanded to ten. After only three and a half years of work, these groups had raised over $20,000, plus the innumerable items they purchased for our kitchen, home, staff, and offices. We encouraged these women to see that this was more than just social work, more than just a group of do-gooders. All auxiliary meetings begin with prayer and devotional readings, for we know we can do nothing without the Lord. These women share our faith in God and commitment to Ranch Hope. Today we have nearly 20 men and women Auxiliaries—each one dedicated to bringing hope to troubled youth.

Wranglers and the Rodeo

Even before the first young people arrived, we made contact with Howard Harris III, who owned and operated a large rodeo in Cowtown. (Started in 1929, it is the oldest rodeo in American with continual performances since that day.) The first rodeo to benefit the Ranch was held the following spring. To the amazement of the owner, we raised over $1,000, thanks to a Ranch Hope men's group called the Wranglers.

Where would we be without the Wranglers? They put together a bowl-a-thon each year and a Golf Tournament, as well as holding a banquet in the spring. At this banquet they present their "Silver Spurs" award, which recognizes the recipient's contribution to one of several categories of youth work. The proceeds from the first rodeo represented the biggest single gift we had received up to that time, and it helped to inspire the men to continue their work.

Don't Leave Home Without It

Kim was a handsome little guy whose mother was

Korean and whose father was an American G.I. His mother had abandoned him as an infant to he brought up in an orphanage. He was adopted by a family in the United States, but was never really accepted by their other children. This, of course, led to big trouble, and Kim rebelled against the family in every way imaginable until he was sent to us. Even at the age of 15, Kim was a ladies' man, and despite his internal turmoil, he was unusually meticulous about his personal appearance and habits.

This debonair kid was really not very charming. He hated the Ranch and used to call it "The Rock," a reference to Alcatraz, the notorious island prison. He mocked me by calling me RH, which for him did not stand for Ranch Hope but "retarded hood." Late one evening I received a call from a local farmer who asked me if a kid carrying a gym bag on a pole was one of mine. After checking, I found out that it was probably Kim and around midnight set out to retrieve him. It was a cold winter night and when I caught up with Kim, I had to negotiate with him to get him to come back with me. I turned up the car heater so he would be sure to get a blast of inviting warm air as he stood outside the window arguing. I guess it worked.

Upon our returning to the cottage, Kim refused to reveal the contents of the gym bag he had taken with him; so I told him he could not go inside until he showed me. Reluctantly, he opened the bag. Now what would you take with you in that bag if you were leaving home on a cold winter's night? Some food, perhaps, or extra clothing? Well, it turned out that this neat freak had only packed aftershave lotion, deodorant, and toilet paper. I guess he felt this made him ready for anything. But the greatest part of the story is that Kim grew up to graduate from the Ranch, was accepted in a nice foster home, and went on to join the U.S. Air Force. Years later, Kim visited Eileen and me with his wife and two lovely kids. He is a career man in the Air Force and doing great. As he was leaving our home, he unexpectedly turned and gave me a big manly hug, "I really love you and appreciate all you did for me, Rev," he said. It touched my heart, and still does, as the battle for lost boys rages on.

Chapter 14

Mid-Life Crisis

By 1988, after almost a quarter century of ministry, Ranch Hope was facing a real dilemma. A declining economy and a couple of years of inadequate fundraising put us in an uncomfortable financial situation. Our facility was less than half filled, and our rates had not increased to reflect the escalating daily costs of housing, treating, feeding, clothing, educating, and otherwise caring for troubled young people. We were not getting as many referrals as we should have from the State Division of Youth and Family Services.

Our low per diem rates were a result of our policy of not accepting state awarded cost-of-living increases due to what had been our great ability to raise funds from private sources. As reports of a national economic downturn gained momentum, many of our previously reliable sources had dried up.

The division (known as DYFS) felt that our program was not designed to accept severely emotionally impaired children, so their referrals were not what they could have been. Enter Jim Whitt! After a disastrous series of events, we had to release the Ranch Hope director who, to say the least, almost destroyed the Ranch. During a period of deep soul searching and seeking God's direction for the future, we consulted a Christian agency, Inter Christo, to help us find a new Director. Interviews were set up with prospective Inter Christo referrals. The process of searching led us to Jim Whitt. Without a doubt from the first moment I met Jim and his wife Barbara, I knew he was the one to lead us out of the wilderness. With academic credentials, experience, and a heart for the Lord's work, the Trustees knew this was the man. After moving onto the campus in Alloway with his four children, Jim at once turned to an immediate need—financial.

Thanks to our new ranch director, we had several meetings with the administrators of the division, including a very helpful supervisor named Barry Silverstein. Initially not much progress was made. You see, to keep the program running and to be able to accept severely emotionally disturbed kids, we needed a substantial infusion of money. It costs a lot to treat these kids because of the additional staff and the special programs that are needed.

Finally we all came up with an idea. If we were agreeable to accepting troubled youth with more serious problems, the division would regionalize our state contract, meaning that instead of having to go through miles of red tape, we would be able to get referrals directly from the district offices of the division in the southern part of New Jersey. This district took in seven counties, which meant that we could regularly consult with the staff of the district offices about the boys they wanted to place and how we could help each boy.

The concept behind this arrangement, which was the first of its kind in New Jersey, was that the district offices had the best idea of the type of boys that needed residential treatment and the level of services required. If a direct negotiation between the district office staff and Ranch Hope was possible, we felt we could build a degree of trust and develop a better service overall for the boys who needed treatment. Limiting the young people we accepted to the southern region instead of the entire state would allow for better communication and a more meaningful engagement.

The negotiations with this agency began with its district offices explicitly defining the population they needed Ranch Hope to serve, as well as the changes in staff and services that would be required to care for these trouble children. Jim Whitt propelled the concept through. As a result of the negotiations, the Ranch geared up to make improvements to accept the tougher cases with funds provided by the state, Surprisingly, we didn't have to "give away the ranch," so to speak. We have retained our Christian identity, while continuing to minister to boys of all races, creeds, and religions. The improved funding has allowed us to attract and retain an even more competent and committed staff, especially child-care staff, which includes house parents and assistants. This staff is now more involved in the care planning process than it was previously. We have established a special cottage to manage young people during periods when they cannot realistically cope with the normal behavior modification system that we mentioned earlier.

Since we developed this new working relationship with the state, we have also been able to more consistently engage the families in the treatment process, Therapists meet more frequently and regularly with the family or family members. A process has also been established that provides for even greater steps than before to avoid releasing one of our youths as a failure. As a result, we have had very few of these so-called negative discharges.

In addition to the frequent communication with the seven district offices, we now meet quarterly with the division's district staff members to review the program and make adjustments when necessary. This arrangement has allowed us to deal with problems when they are small and maintain the overall spirit of mutual cooperation. From Ranch Hope's perspective, this is a relationship that works. It came at a time when facilities like ours were straining under the pressure of a sharp drop in private contributions. It has allowed us to continue to live in the world and still maintain our divine principles, to render unto God that which is God's and unto Caesar that which is Caesar's.

Speaking from the state's perspective, this is how Barry Silverstein reported on the success of the new relationship in a statewide newsletter three years after it began:

> Overall the results of our efforts have been very gratifying. Ranch Hope has been serving the (really troubled youth), the southern region district offices have been very satisfied with the services provided. Ranch Hope has been operating at near a 100 percent occupancy, and children and families involved are receiving a needed service.

This partnership with the state is unusual, and we thank God that we have been able to maintain our Christian foundations and practices while also being able to serve our community by accepting even more boys that desperately need help. In many ways the Ranch is a poster child for faith-based initiative. Long before it became something for political debate, we were practicing it successfully. It is a win/win situation.

Chapter 15

Hope for Dead-End Kids

By 2002, the nation's state and federal prison and local jail population exceeded 2 million for the first time in history, according to the Bureau of Justice statistics.[25] This is a rate of 702 prisoners per 100,000 population and costs us $20,000 or more per inmate. The only nation that even comes close is Russia, with less than half the amount of inmates, but a rate of 602 prisoners per 100,000 population.

As you can imagine, these statistics have attracted a lot of media attention. The news story that really blew my mind appeared in *The New York Times*. Looking at the rise in the incarceration rate and crime in general, the story quoted a west coast sociologist who asserted that it was quite an interesting mystery "why the United States was the most violent nation on earth."[25] As

Christians treating the kids who otherwise would become part of the above statistics—and some who do anyway—there is no mystery in our minds concerning the frightening numbers.

We know why there is so much hatred and violence. We know that hurting people hurt other people. It is a sad game of pass-it-along. The pain of our children becomes the pain of their children and their spouses, and more and more others outside the family. How can this chain of hurt be broken? Can it be broken at all? Well, there is a good chance it can. After first laying a bit of groundwork, I hope to show you how hurt kids get healed, and what it takes.

Luke on the Lost

Summarizing how young people become troubled, I like to use the three "lost" parables in Luke 16 that we mentioned in the beginning of the book. I would just like to add a little something to better illustrate the analogy. The first is the parable of the lost sheep, which became lost through its own carelessness. It put its head down, started nibbling, and finally roamed away from the flock and the shepherd. It got careless. In more than four decades of working with troubled youth, we've seen that some have become careless like that sheep—careless at home, in school, on the streets. They became distracted, started nibbling on the wrong things in life, and got lost from where they should have been. Remember what the shepherd did? He didn't blame the sheep and leave it to its own demise. He went out and searched for it, leaving the other 99 ones safely behind. When he finally found the lost one, he rejoiced.

The lost coin parable is a bit different. It involved a woman who lost one of her ten coins. Over the years we've had young people who were lost because of somebody else—the carelessness of parents, teachers, society, drug pushers, or other adults who abused them in some way. My wife Eileen recalls one of the first boys we worked with in our home before the Ranch was built. His name was Jack. One night Jack was being stopped by his mother from going out drinking with his pals. But Jack wouldn't hear it. He beat the poor woman unmercifully on her face, arms, and stomach. The next day, we saw her, and she was black and blue and purple all over. He had struck her again and again and again.

Of course there is no justification whatsoever for any young person striking a parent or anyone else. But you know, there was a time in that young man's life when he was very spiritual and even wanted to study for the priesthood? He was an altar boy in his church. What happened? Well, he had a drunken father, one who never went to church and who set a horrible example. So there came a time when Jack said, "If my old man doesn't go to church and treat people right, why should I?"

Sometimes through the carelessness of adults, our young people drift away from where they should be and become lost like that coin. But the good woman in the parable, if you recall, did not say "so what" and forget about the coin because she had nine more. Instead, she feverishly swept the floor of her house and searched and searched until she found the coin. When she did, she called her neighbors over to celebrate. I like to celebrate and rejoice at Ranch Hope every time we find a lost boy, lost because of someone else's carelessness.

Finally, there was the prodigal son, a lost son—and from a good home, too. He had no particular reason to abruptly leave home and family, but he did. He had a brother with whom he possibly did not get along, but his parents were all right. One of the interesting things about the story of the son was that the father had no other recourse but to sit home and wait and pray for his son's return.

One of the boys who was here some time ago, Rick, did fine for the entire three years he was at the ranch and at Hope Home, but he did not do well when he left. He was in and out of prison. Finally he got a good factory job with a big corporation in California. He settled down and got married. Although his marriage was not without its rough spots for the first four years, Rick eventually was so successful that he gained a couple of rapid promotions. He and his wife had a little girl and saved a nice nest egg, with which they moved back to the Philadelphia area to be closer to his brothers and sisters. Rick surprised me one night by just showing up at my door while Eileen and I were having dessert at the dinner table. I was thrilled to see him. The next night he, his wife, and their six-year-old daughter came over for dinner, and we had a great time reminiscing and praising God for the blessings in his life and ours. My point here is that, like the prodigal, sometimes all that Papa Bailey can do is sit home and wait and pray for a son to return. Most often, as in Rick's case, this requires a surrendering of one's life and will to our Lord and Master, Jesus Christ, while trusting in Him for the results.

Sometimes the staff of Ranch Hope has tried everything to help a boy, but he still rebels. It seems he has to go out and wallow around in the pig slop a little longer before finally getting the message. I had to sit and wait for Rick. Others, praise God, change right here. Still others have to go back out and see how bad things can be before they truly surrender.

Joseph was one of the Ranch Hope boys who will never know how much better his life could have been if he had followed the Lord Jesus. Joseph held up a liquor store one night when he was 19 and was met by an off-duty cop as he was about to make his getaway. The cop shouted at Joseph to stop and put his hands up. Joseph got off a shot, but the officer's shot was the only one that found its mark. Joseph died instantly. There was no cause for celebration with Joseph like there was with Rick. Rick was the rebellious son who came home; Joseph never made it, I often recall these Bible verses as I drive onto our campus, pondering the progress of young people such as these. The Lord has blessed us with many examples of how the staff of Ranch Hope has searched for, cared about, and waited for boys and girls who eventually had their lives turn out for the good.

Needy Kids Need More

In researching this book, one of the extraordinary things that Lee Carney and I came across was the recommendation by secular layman in the federal government that churches "must become involved in helping parents to teach their children to respect themselves and others."[27]

Well, that's a good start. It's a simple but important recommendation that should inspire us to hold gatherings of child-care providers throughout the country to discuss how to recruit our churches to serve parents in this way. Ranch Hope certainly would be open to host such a meeting on a regional basis.

The larger solution as I see it, however, goes deeper than handing over the responsibility for teaching proper parenting to individual churches. The responsibility for properly rearing children can only be learned from God through the churches. And in order for hurting parents with hurting kids to change their lives and to learn and teach mutual respect, their lives must be given over in willing submission to Jesus Christ.

We know that the discussion we've had in this book

on divorce, sexual immorality, abortion, occultism, crime, and violence are all definite signs that our society has collectively decided that God will not rule and have His way.

Sadly, we are a nation that has turned its back on God. We can trace this rejection back many years to the beginnings of the dissolution of the American family and the decided decline in the moral standards that we, as a nation, had held sacred and dear throughout most of the previous two and a half centuries.

Churches by themselves can do little to reverse this generational curse as long as parents don't recognize the authority of God in the churches. Each hurting adult's seeds of rebellion, rejection, and anger are brought into his or her marriage. The seeds germinate and keep the pain budding, proliferating in each new generation.

I am optimistic that the Christian renewal we're seeing in some regions of our land, especially among those in their teens and early 20s, is a sign that God and His Church are coming against the spirit of agnosticism and the moral collapse of our society. It will, nevertheless, be a battle all the way; and we, as Christians, are called as soldiers to fight it. It's true that the weapons of our warfare are not carnal or physical; they are instead weapons of prayer and fasting and spiritual action. God will stand on the front lines and fight the battle for us, but God only goes where He is wanted. He does not force himself on an individual or a nation. We must allow Him to lead.

In addition, our job as Christians is to establish places where God feels at home and to offer spiritual hospitality to those who are lost and wounded. We need to show them God's neighborhood, God's forgiveness. We must become a real demonstration of His love.

A New Vision

A few years ago were privileged to hear an old bishop from Oklahoma who was part native American. He told us a story one night at a preaching mission about his wandering through an ancient cemetery in his home state and discovering a pyramid-shaped tombstone. Well, that's a pretty fascinating tombstone for those parts, and the bishop, a huge man of about 250 pounds, knelt to read the inscription.

On one of the three inscribed sides of the pyramid was written, "Of the Past, Be Mindful." The bishop shifted to the second side, which said, "To the Present, Be Faithful," And then the third side, which read, "For the Future, Be Hopeful." This story puts things in perspective for the future of Ranch Hope, The Bible promises us that the Lord's plans for us are for good, not evil, and that He will provide a good and hopeful future for those who love and obey His Word. The Bible also says we must have a vision or we will perish.

Being the Christian home and neighborhood that we are, we don't want members of our family to ever feel abandoned because they left the Ranch and we didn't care anymore. A person is not abandoned in a healthy Christian family, and we want the Ranch to be even more of a refuge and haven than it has been.

For both boys and girls who have had a taste of right living at the Ranch but are, keep in mind, still emotionally disturbed or emotionally immature, returning to their old environments can cause them to revert to old, maladaptive behaviors and addictions. It is our prayer to provide them with a place where they can, as the old poem by the unknown author says, rest if they must, "but don't you quit." Part of that rhyme also says that "You never can tell how close you are (to succeeding); it may be near when it seems so far." Our God is the Lord of the second chance, and we want our group homes and half-way houses to be places of encouragement as troubled boys and girls take another shot at life after failing.

Confirmation of this part of our vision was seen in one boy who left the Ranch after five years. He did a stint in the military, but when he got out he could not hold down a job and live successfully without an institutional-like structure. We took him in at the age of 27 and gave him a custodial job here. After six months, his spirit was lifted, and he's now talking about attending a county college nearby and eventually getting into law enforcement work. We now know what a few months more of Ranch Hope can do for someone.

Let's Get Going

The 18th century preacher and evangelist John Wesley once said that the world was his parish. I've reversed that by declaring that my parish (Ranch Hope) is my world. I hope it's not too much of a disappointment to some of you if I say that Dave Bailey *does not* have a world vision. However, I *do have* a vision for troubled youth. I believe that the Lord is waiting for others to replicate what He's allowed us to accomplish here. And I feel strongly that the purpose of this book is to share our experience and hope with the Christian Community, urging the brethren to set up their own Ranch Hope in their very own mission fields. We have solidly established the need—there is no ignoring the startling statistics on juvenile delinquency and the terrible warnings about the decade of violence in which we are living.

My plea to fellow Christians is, "Let's get going! Let's get started!" We are always learning at the Ranch, but our four decades of God-given wisdom and knowledge are waiting to be shared with everyone as more and more people look toward our program as a possible model. I've been asked, along with others on our professional staff, to serve as a consultant to those who want to establish a residential treatment facility or revamp their existing operation with fresh new programs and ideas. I think that pastors, child-care providers, churches, and entire communities need to look around at the great need and ask themselves if the way in which their community, their country, or their region is helping troubled kids is really working. More and more, Ranch Hope is bringing what we have learned out into the surrounding community and beyond. We have had the benefit of experiencing many trials and we have known many good counselors, and we desire to openly share what Cod has shown us.

Chapter 16

The Seed That Fell on Fertile Soil

A young woman first planted the seed at an evangelistic meeting in a small borough in Southern New Jersey. Thirty years ago, I had the opportunity to conduct a week of services at Pitman Grove in Pitman, New Jersey. The town of Pitman was actually established around the campground. Near the turn of the 19th century, members of the Methodist Church set up a summer camp inside a large grove of oak trees. At first it was the traditional "camp meeting" with tents erected around an area called the tabernacle. Preaching services were held each summer, and people came by train and horse-drawn carriage to spend time studying the Word and hearing revivalist preaching.

Between 1900 and World War I, the camp grew considerably, and soon, people began building permanent residences around the site. It was on this site that many believe Austin Miles penned the beautiful hymn, "In the Garden."

Even today, Pitman's population is less than 14,000, so the odds of the events that happened that summer night were not skewed by an uncommonly large group of people. Divine Providence was at work, and even though the seed lay dormant for many years, it did not die.

After the service on that warm July evening, a young woman came forward and handed me a letter. "Please take this letter, Rev. Bailey, and read it as soon as you can." I placed the envelope in my Bible with my notes from the service.

"Thanks for coming tonight. I'll be much in prayer for you," I said as she hurried out of the tabernacle. I never saw her again and have no idea her name or where she lives. But as soon as I arrived home, I opened the envelope very prayerfully. Inside was the story of her life.

The narrative was disturbing. It told of her experiences growing up in a troubled household. She spoke of her broken family, her difficult school experiences, and her damaged relationships. She ended the letter with these pointed words: "Reverend Bailey, I hope that one day you'll start a home for girls. I have heard about the work you are doing with boys at Ranch Hope, but I believe there are also a number of girls out here who need your help." This teenage girl opened my eyes to a great need, but little did I realize that it would take 20 years for the seed to germinate, or that it would be nearly three decades before the idea would grow to fruition.

The boys at Ranch Hope were enthusiastic about the idea of bringing a group of girls to the Alloway campus. They even pointed out a natural divide in the 100-acre property that would keep each gender safely isolated on either side of a 50-yard wide marsh. One boy said, "Look Rev, it's a natural. Put the girls on one side of the marsh, and we'd be on the other side." I said, "Sure. And I can hear it every night from about eleven o'clock on…splash, whoosh, splash. You guys would be sloshing through the marsh to be with the girls, or the girls would be working their way through the bog to get to you. In fact, you'd probably build pontoon bridges to get to each other."

Even though the guys were excited about the idea, many of my friends and colleagues warned me of the many difficulties and challenges that would occur if we set up a home for troubled girls on the same property with boys. So with that wise advice running through my mind, I decided that, although there was a need to start a work for girls, I could not put both boys and girls on the same campus, even if they were separated by a marsh. Also, there was the huge factor of financing a new program at this time. We were still struggling to maintain the boys' ministry. Everything would be put on hold, trusting God's timing into the future. Little did I realize the waiting period would stretch more than twenty years.

Sometime back in the 1970s, I was introduced to Bob Smith. Bob was a building contractor and an active Christian layman. After he came to know the Lord, he was led to use his talents to reach young people. So, by the mid 70s, Bob and his wife Joan founded a ministry for girls they called Nikos Academy. The word *nikos* is the Greek word used in the sports brand "Nike," and means "victory," so essentially, the ministry was called "Victory Academy." The Smiths spent many years helping girls in distressing home situations and dedicated much time and energy to Nikos Academy, then located in Glassboro, New Jersey.

The Smiths came to the attention of Ranch Hope in an unusual way. Each year an auxiliary support group called the Wranglers sponsors a banquet. The Wranglers are men who provide a positive role model for our youth as well as raise funds through various projects. Their motto reflects each man's commitment, "A Wrangler's help is a boy's hope." At the annual banquet, someone is honored for his or her work with troubled youth. Usually, the men search for an unsung hero. It was in 1975 that the Wranglers received a letter recommending the Smiths for their work at Nikos Academy. It was a unanimous decision to honor Bob and Joan Smith with the award called the "Silver Spurs." A relationship was now solidified that would lead to answered prayer.

God continued to bless Nikos Academy, and shortly after Bob and his wife received the Wrangler award, the facility moved to Williamstown, New Jersey. The program became a self-contained unit, complete with a school, counseling services and over 30 rooms to house the 10 girls who lived there.

Years passed, and the ministry flourished, but eventually, the time came when Bob and his wife realized that the work was becoming too much for them to handle. Mrs. Smith had a mini stroke and became physically unable to meet the demands of Nikos Academy. So one day I got a phone call from Bob.

"Dave, my wife and I think it's time to move on. But we want Nikos to continue, and the bottom line is that we want Ranch Hope to take over." I was stunned, to say the least.

It took me a moment to respond. "Wow! That sounds great! I've always wanted to expand the Ranch to help girls, but there is a big problem. We are not in a good position now financially, Bob. I don't think it will be possible...."

"Wait a minute, Dave. I'm not calling to offer you a financial proposition. 1 want you to take over Nikos—no cost."

There IS a Difference!

When we took over Nikos Academy, all of the girls the Smiths had previously worked with were gone. We did a few minor renovations to the house, but basically, everything was there to begin our work. That was the easy part.

As news spread about the new project, someone asked me, "Dave do you know what you're getting into? Girls are," he cautioned, "a different breed—an entity to themselves." And to be honest, I did not know what we were getting into. But then again, I had no idea what was in store for me back in 1962 when we started the work with boys. I have often said that I was glad the Lord got me when I was young and dumb. Otherwise, doubt might have overcome my vision, and Ranch Hope may never have started.

In the period before the girls came to live in Nikos House, I spoke in the city of Cape May Court House, New Jersey. I talked about our dream for the work with girls and how God was making that dream a reality. After the message, an elderly woman approached me with a stern look in her eyes. "Rev. Bailey," she said, "I heard you talk tonight about starting a home for girls. Let me tell you something. I taught school for 40 years and believe me, there *is* a difference between boys and girls. When girls get angry, they scratch, pull hair, and sink their teeth into your skin. I believe you're biting off more than you can chew if you start working with girls."

In reality, I appreciated her input, as well as the counsel of dozens of others. However, the need to help girls was there, and suddenly we had this miracle dropped in our lap. It was time to launch into another important dimension of helping troubled youth.

In the fall of 1995, we formally opened our girls' facility. There was a minor change in its name from Nikos Academy to Nikos House. We wanted to give it a new identity while keeping some semblance of its past. Also, we decided to eliminate the "in house" school and instead send the girls to a local high school. There was also to be a greater emphasis on counseling and more staff would be involved. A treatment team would begin to work with the girls in a group home setting.

Unfortunately, the behavior modification program was ineffective, since the girls were away most of the day in public school. They tended to hang out with other students who had severe problems and would run away from school, cause disruptions in the classroom, and try to bring boys back to the house. We soon realized that we had to come up with an alternative to sending the girls into the community each day.

We also found that the girls responded more emotionally to the program than the boys did. When they became angry with each other, they did not react with the quick physical aggression of the boys. They plotted, schemed, and stole from each other, holding onto their anger and drawing out their revenge for a long time. Since the girls were, indeed, proving to be completely different individuals than the boys, we knew that we would have to adapt our strategies and rearrange our program to better address their needs. We added more staff, including therapists, to work more closely with the girls.

Even the setting of the two campuses was different.

The boys were located in a rural setting, away from people and businesses. The girls were in a rural setting, also, but were located in the suburbs of Williamstown, New Jersey, close to major highways and public transportation. That made it easier for them to find ways to get into town, and consequently to get into trouble. But, as problems arose, solutions came as well, and in the process, we all learned and grew.

We changed the name of the facility from Nikos Academy to Victory House. It seemed to be easier for people to remember "victory" than "nikos," although they both essentially mean the same thing. In fact, we like to remind our girls that the name "Nicodemus" also comes from the root word "nikos." We tell them how Jesus changed the life of Nicodemus and encourage them to allow Jesus to change their lives, as well.

So far, we have helped more than 200 girls. Not all of them, of course, have been rehabilitated and redeemed, but a large percentage of them have. We have a wonderful chaplain who visits the girls, helps them in their spiritual growth, and conducts Sunday morning worship. We also take the girls to Christian concerts and retreats. They are allowed to go shopping, celebrate the holidays with special parties, and to grow as young women in Christ.

Quoting one of our staff, "They have been a handful!" But our Victory House supervisor, Mary DiDonna, shared the following exciting stories that encourage us to keep the faith.

1. Carol was picked up as a runaway. She refused to go home and threatened to commit suicide if returned home. She was placed at Victory House but was rejected by her family throughout her Victory House stay. Despite the lack of family support, she maintained a Level 2 most of the time. After a year and three months, Carol left Victory House. She has since received her high school diploma, maintained a job at WalMart, and recently joined the Air Force, a dream she had expressed since her arrival at Victory House.

2. Judy found herself placed at Victory House because of self-mutilating, homicidal and suicidal gesturing, running away, and drug usage. Judy did not get along with her mother. After 15 months, Judy was discharged to her stepmother and father. Half a year later, we heard she was doing fine and attending Midway School. She and her stepmother and father were enjoying their new relationships and experiencing a good family life.

3. With a history of "stubbornness and resistance to authority" as well as running away, Kathy was depressed and suicidal when she was admitted to Victory House. After 22 months, Kathy went home with her adoptive mother. More than a year later, Kathy is involved in high school sports and has a "B" average in school. Kathy and her mother are starting a business together and have become active with a Ranch Hope Auxiliary.

One of our young women has gone into the military through the Air Force's ROTC program. Others choose to go to college or to begin to take their place in the work force. The staff at Victory House is there to encourage, uplift, and to train these teenagers in the way they should go. They are there to facilitate the transition between Victory House and the "real world," helping to deal with family relationships, social problems, and spiritual challenges.

Midway School

As I mentioned before, one of the great needs of the girls at Victory House was an educational facility that did not involve our relinquishing supervision to the community each day. We needed a self-contained resource that would allow us to educate the girls, while at the same time maintaining our behavioral modification program. None of the staff at Victory House felt called to be home school educators, but, as it turns out, God had another miracle in store.

In 2004, we celebrated the 48th anniversary of our radio program, "The Wondrous Story." Actually, this program helped us in the formative days of the Ranch. Many people first heard of Ranch Hope through the radio broadcasts over local stations. "The Wondrous Story" is a three-dimensional outreach: it features an audio news magazine discussing signs of the times, a musical segment, and a devotional message. In between sections, we talk about our work at the Ranch.

One day, I received a phone call from a couple who

listened to our radio program on a regular basis. Julie and Joe Air were the founders of a Special Education school in Lumberton, New Jersey called Midway School. The school accepted students through the eighth grade, helping special needs children to be taught in a structured educational environment.

Midway School met in an old Nike base. Back in the 60s, Philadelphia had a string of Nike Bases around it. In case of a military attack, these Nike missiles would bring down any enemy plane that might fly into the area. As the threat of attack lessened, these bases were basically abandoned and sold by the government. Julie and Joe bought one of them and converted it into a school. For many years they ministered to special needs children— emotionally disturbed and academically challenged students.

Julie and Joe began the relationship by asking Ranch Hope to assist them with their supervisory needs. In order to remain accredited by the State of New Jersey, they needed a principal. We agreed to permit our principal, Dr. Charles Hawn, to go to Midway two days a week and supervise Ranch Hope three days a week. This provided both schools with the administration needed to keep their academic standing.

The Airs eventually felt that God was calling them to move on. Their biggest concern, of course, was finding a Christian organization to take over Midway School. Enter Ranch Hope. One day, Joe called Dr. Hawn into his office for some startling news. "Julie and I think it's time for a change. We have considered some alternatives and have decided to ask Ranch Hope to maintain our ministry at Midway." Dr. Hawn couldn't contain his enthusiasm. "I'll be in touch with the Rev tomorrow and give you his reaction."

When Dr. Hawn asked me if I had any interest, it was like asking a little boy if he'd like a puppy! Of course we were interested! Not only was it a new way to minister to needy children, it was also a place we could send our girls to school! Midway School was only about 30 minutes by bus from Williamstown, New Jersey. It was a marriage made in heaven! Within one year, Julie and Joe fazed themselves out of the program and moved to Louisiana. Ranch Hope was soon completely in charge of Midway School. We are ministering to nearly 50 students each day in this school for special education students.

Midway School is a beautiful location in the suburbs of Lumberton, New Jersey. It spans 10 acres and allows us to offer a wide range of activities for the students including indoor and outdoor sports, special interest classes such as cooking and woodworking, counseling and excellent academic training. Praise God for another miracle!

Chapter 17

A Bad Apple

For a number of years, Ranch Hope wanted to start a summer camp. The idea fit into our "circle of care," a standard we have created to address different dimensions of youth work. One of our concerns was the fact that there were kids out there who simply needed a week away from home—young people from inner cities, suburbs, or the country, whose families couldn't afford to send them to summer camp. There might also be church kids who would benefit from time at a Christian camp.

Our first thought was to construct the camp right here on our campus at Ranch Hope in Alloway. The entire campus spanned 130 acres bordering a beautiful lake, perfect for a summer campground. Administrative duties would also be simpler if the works were geographically connected. Eight weeks out of every summer, Ranch Hope would set aside time for campers to join us and benefit from our time together.

We went through a long series of meetings with architects, and one of those architects made a lasting impression on our administrative staff. "We are impressed with this man; his credentials make him just the architect to help us." Little did I realize those words spoken at a board meeting would come back to haunt me.

After a couple of phone calls and some correspondence he made his first visit and spent time outlining plans for the summer campground, complete with a large lodge to house year-round activities. We spent a great deal of time and money working with him, and he finally produced a blueprint for a grandiose structure, one that would cost about a half million dollars. "This really is more than we can afford," I said awkwardly. But he was quick to respond, "You must plan not only for today, but for the future. My plans will help take you into the 21st century."

Obviously, our budget was not equipped to handle such a proposition, and it's probably just as well, because we found out later that the guy wasn't really an architect. He was not even licensed in the State of New Jersey for any work. All of the blueprints he had drawn were unlawful and illegitimate. We could do nothing but release him and scrap the plans.

That unfortunate experience did not erase the

dream. It was just as real and vivid as before. But our economic resources simply weren't adequate to build the kind of campground that he had envisioned, so we put the idea away in our mental file.

Things Are Not Always What They Seem

Many years ago, before Ranch Hope was started, a Methodist minister friend began a very popular youth camp, which he conducted every summer in central New Jersey. After a number of years, he decided that it was time for his ministry and vision to change direction, and he made plans to sell the camp. Since the site had been part of the Southern New Jersey Methodist Conference for years, arrangements for the sale were made by the Conference. Trustees were appointed to search for a ministry to take over the camp; a ministry that would closely follow the values and principles the minister had taught. The search committee eventually found its way to Ranch Hope.

"Dave, this is Bill Thielking. I'm calling for the Conference. We have a camp I thought you would be interested in, and we think Ranch Hope and this camp ministry are a perfect match. When can we talk?" (Rev. Bill Thielking was chairman of the Trustee Committee.)

I held the phone in disbelief, but finally responded, "You have to be kidding! Let's meet soon!" Within two weeks we were on our way to a new location about one hour from the Ranch. The campground was in good shape, the location was great, and it seemed as though the Lord was answering our prayers in a specific way. We thought it might be the Ranch Hope summer camp.

It took a number of months of negotiation. The Ranch had saved money for the building of a camp facility, but this one came with everything constructed and ready to open. I made the proposal to our Ranch Hope Board of Managers. "We can offer $350,000 to the Conference and, hopefully, it will be accepted." A unanimous vote of the Board sealed the deal, and we contacted the Conference Trustees. I was more than excited when I called Bill.

"Everything is go," I almost shouted into the phone. "We'll wait to hear from you."

Bill was nearly as excited as I was, and closed the conversation with the statement, "It's just a matter of the Conference approving our report, and you have the camp!"

That very summer, we met with the Conference in Southern New Jersey and decided that Ranch Hope would purchase the camp. I came home from the meeting elated. The buildings and grounds were well maintained, and we saw no reason why we couldn't open the campground the following summer. There were no warning bells going off in my head, no red flags flying. As far as I could see, this was a direct affirmation from the Lord.

On the Friday after the conference, I called a friend, Reverend Jim Doran, and told him how thrilled we were about the camp. After a long pause, he said, "Oh Dave, you missed something. After you left, they called together a special session and rescinded their decision. They felt that Ranch Hope did not offer them enough money, and they accepted an offer from the Boy Scouts who agreed to give them double what Ranch Hope offered." The extra money would provide scholarships for worthy children at another Conference sponsored camp site.

I didn't know how to respond. It had seemed so perfect from the start—a match made in heaven. The Conference's decision sent shock waves through the entire Ranch Hope community. Although the Boy Scouts are a worthy organization and do an excellent job of teaching boys life skills, they are not an evangelical Christian group and are limited as to what they can do with religious programming. Needless to say, we were concerned that the Conference had decided to bypass an evangelical ministry in favor of a secular organization who happened to have more financial resources at its disposal. But the decision was made, and our dream of a summer camp went down the tubes.

After that experience with the Methodist Conference, we decided that perhaps we would again consider a small camp program built on the Ranch property. After all, we had plenty of space on the Alloway campus, and one of our open fields bordered a beautiful lake. It would also be easier to administer. Many of the facilities and activities could overlap with our boys' work; for instance, use of the horse program, the pool, the cafeteria for eating, other buildings for crafts, and recreation in the gymnasium. Once again, on paper it looked like a great idea. An architect friend, Leroy Davis, who had helped us from the start of the Ranch, suggested, "Dave, this could be a wilderness camp. The kids could really rough it all summer, and you would have a minimum of costs for buildings and camp sites." It didn't take much to convince me, and our energy was now directed to improving the lakefront and starting a wilderness camp.

Well, the Lord never said it would he easy. Remember Jesus' words, "In this world you will have tribulation..." Enter the tribulation...again!

Now, you would think sewage would not be a big problem with a wilderness camp, but think again. It was THE big problem. The State of New Jersey laws required such a large system for showers, toilets, and kitchen waste that we were looking at $100,000 in costs. (Johnnys-on-the-Spot were not acceptable.) "Fold up the tents, gang. Let's go back to the drawing board. Bye-bye Wilderness Camp." That was the most I could say as the county engineer read the death sentence.

A Dollar Buys a Lot These Days

All of us have had the experience of calling someone

on the phone and being placed on hold. That is exactly how I felt as I waited for the Lord's next move in regards to the summer camp. Surprise! Surprise! A big MOVE was coming!

Just about a mile from our Alloway campus was an old Boy Scout Camp (not the Boy Scouts again!). In 1930, the Atlantic Area Boy Scout Council of America bought Camp Edge after selling another camp in Pennsylvania. The name was chosen to honor a New Jersey Governor, Walter B. Edge, who had served from 1917-1919. The camp had once been an old mill with a lake whose water was used to generate power for the mill. Through the years, the Scouts had erected buildings and improved the property. Eventually, they owned 250 acres of land, a lake, and many beautiful campsites.

When we arrived in Alloway back in 1962, the camp was still in use, but little by little, because of increased costs of maintenance, the Atlantic Area Boy Scouts phased out their work at Camp Edge. Even with this knowledge, I was totally surprised when the Scouts called me from their Central Office and said, "Rev. Dave, we understand Ranch Hope wants to begin a summer camp. The Boy Scouts would like to sell you Camp Edge..."

I didn't respond for a moment. In my mind I was thinking, Is this weird? Have we come full circle? Finally, I blurted out, "Yep, we're more than interested in a summer camp. What do you have in mind?" I should not have asked that question. In the next two minutes, I felt a panic attack coming on.

"Camp Edge is for sale, and we're asking $850,000—a real deal for such a great site." A real deal? Not for us; not at that price. How do you graciously tell someone that we appreciate the offer but haven't struck oil yet? It didn't take long to state just that, not in those terms, of course.

"As much as we like Camp Edge, and though it could be ideal for us, I must say no. It is well out of our reach."

There was no room for arbitration, so another door was slammed shut, or so I thought.

Fasten Your Spiritual Seat Belts

Several years later, another phone call came. The State of New Jersey wanted to talk with us about our summer camp idea. Because of our relationship with the Department of Youth and Family Services and other State agencies, word had filtered down about our interest. Enter Green Acres. Green Acres is an environmental organization. It serves as a type of real estate agent for the Department of Environmental Protection, purchasing land that becomes part of the system of state parks, forests, natural and wildlife management areas. The Green Acres representative bombed us with, "Rev. Bailey, we are planning to buy Camp Edge..." I thought to myself, *So? What does that mean to us?* But he quickly added, "We're looking for someone to manage the camp for us, improve it, and use it for camping or any other program that will benefit the community."

And... and... and..., I thought. He finally arrived at the blockbuster, "The State of New Jersey will lease it to you for 15 years at one dollar a year."

Disbelief is a mild way to describe my reaction. Of course we were interested. Where do we sign? We went from $850,000 to $15 (do you like the math?) with a fifteen-year lease and the option to renew at the end of 15 years. YES! YES! Now we could use our reserve funds, not to purchase property, but to improve an existing camp. Remember the verse I quoted earlier from the lips of Jesus? "In the world you will have tribulation..." Now I could complete it: "...but I have overcome the world." Again, I realized His grace made me an overcomer! We would soon begin the process of renovating the Ranger's house, the cafeteria, the boat house, the lodge, lake, docks, and all the camp sites. It was suddenly within our grasp to consummate the dream. And, praise God, the camp is now open for summer use, weekend retreats, and year-round camping.

Oh, did I forget to mention that thrown into the mix was a ropes course? We now call it "Project Outdoor Challenge." It is a course to help people (young and old) to work together through a series of physical challenges like climbing ropes, walking planks, scaling walls, sliding down cables, and a myriad of initiative games. This was a bonus feature of Camp Edge I didn't know existed.

Already hundreds of people have come to test their skills. In 2004, our first year of summer camp, we ministered to more than 400 underprivileged boys and girls. Our Lord also provided a couple to live on the campus and manage this new dimension of Ranch Hope. Thank God for Jack and Sue Fosbenner.

The Circle Widens—HILLS Program

We have talked about the "Circle of Care," and our circle of care has increased from the original Boy's Ranch to the Girl's Ranch to a group home on the site called Hope Home. It also includes the special education school, Midway, and now, Camp Edge, our summer camp for young people. There was one other area in the Circle of Care that we had discussed years ago at a retreat for our Board of Managers at Sandy Cove Bible Conference Center—an independent living program we call HILLS (Hope for Independent Living and Life Skills). We decided to offer an independent living option to young men who graduated from the Ranch or who were attending a vocational school, working, going to college, or just needed a place to live temporarily. This program has a much less structured environment, and the young people do their own household chores cooking, laundry, money management, etc.

We had four cottages on the Ranch, which were not in use by staff, so we converted them into independent living facilities for the young men. They live, work, or go to vocational school while maintaining a residence on

Ranch property. These young men are learning essential life management skills with the help of the HILLS program. We have a person on staff to help with vocational training, and we provide transportation to and from work. Our boys have worked in local restaurants, industries, and companies, and some of them work directly on the Ranch. We are hoping to eventually have twelve boys in the HILLS program. This requires a staff that can provide case management, life skills training, and mentoring. Employment training is very important to these young people as we prepare them to compete and succeed in today's work environment.

Shelter of Hope

For years we had wanted to have a place to meet the needs of children who did not need long-term placement: children who had family problems, were runaways, victims of domestic violence, or were awaiting foster home placement. After almost a year of negotiating with our local government officials, the Salem County Freeholders, a contract was signed for the Shelter of Hope. Finally in the summer of 2004, the Shelter of Hope was opened on two of our campuses. Our former administration building at the Ranch was converted to a place of care and blessing where ten boys can be temporarily cared for. Six girls are being helped at Victory House.

So you can see that our tasks have not always been

clearly defined or easy to carry out. There have been (and certainly will continue to be) times that we "walk by faith and not by sight." But we always keep in mind the fact that the Lord rewards faithfulness, and it is our goal to always remain faithful to Him and to the work which He has called us to do.

On Sunday, July 1, 2004, the Ranch reached another milestone—Dave Jr. and I switched positions. At a beautiful service of succession in our chapel, Dave became the Executive Director of the Ranch and I became Director of Development. During the service I passed the mantle of leadership to the next generation. Like Elijah praying for Elisha, I laid hands on Dave in the Lee Ann Bailey Memorial Chapel. Many family, friends, and staff joined us at the altar. I spoke about the important words that had sustained me in the past and would help Dave into the future as Executive Director.

"Stay focused, stay faithful, and always finish the courses" were my three recommendations that will provide a foundation for the young man who was born and raised on the Ranch and after college returned to work with us. He has ministered as child care worker, coach for our athletic teams, administrator, fundraiser, and has taken on any other position where there was a need. He is well prepared to lead us into the next phase of the Ranch ministry.

Chapter 18

Forgiveness and Hope

The vision behind our day-to-day operation of Ranch Hope is to break the chain of pain. Troubled, hurting kids are kids that have been offended. The offenses may take the form of rejection and lack of love, of physical and sexual abuse. They may have been committed against them by parents, other adults, society at large, or even themselves. Sometimes an unloved boy is so vulnerable that he becomes his own worst enemy. As Christians we have the key that can unlock the prison of rage and revenge and replace it with the liberty of love. The key is forgiveness.

The Word of God tells us we must forgive others or our Father in heaven will not forgive us. That's often easier said than done, of course, especially for a troubled boy who has been batted around for his first dozen years or more. It's possible, though, and it's a commandment, not an option, if we want to be cleansed and made whole.

I like what pastor and author Charles Stanley of Atlanta says about the tragedy of the spirit of unforgiveness. It can take up residence in us in childhood and linger with us to the grave and beyond if we let it. That tragedy, he says in his book *The Gift of Forgiveness,*

> ...is the bondage people find themselves in which they do not grasp the immensity of God's forgiveness. It is a bondage that stifles their ability to love and accept those they know in their hearts most deserve their love. It is a bondage that cripples marriages from their outset. It is a bondage that is often passed from generation to generation. it is a bondage that chokes out the abundant life of Christ promised to those who would believe."[28]

I agree with Stanley. Only by understanding God's forgiveness and making it a conscious part of our lives can we be delivered from this bondage. There is great motivation to break out of the bondage of unforgiveness, as the Bible tells us in many ways. You see, the real loser is you, "The person who has an unforgiving spirit is always the real loser," Stanley says, "much more so than the one against whom the grudge is held. This is easy to see when we take a closer look at the things most people withhold from those they feel have wronged them." Unforgiveness, the author explains, "by its very nature prevents individuals from following through on many of the specifics of the Christian life and practically necessitates that they walk by the flesh rather than by the spirit."

Wise men have extracted formulas from the Bible for forgiving those they feel have offended and rejected them. Without calling it a formula, forgiveness is really what we try to teach our young people here. We tell them the guy who forgives is a winner and is blessed. He becomes liberated and able to go on with his life—to live and to love. Our greatest joy comes when young people find acceptance in Christ, realize the extent of Christ's love for them, and learn what it means to forgive and to love. They becomes different creatures, and the old things become new. Through the grace of Almighty God and the forgiveness and acceptance of His loving Son, Jesus Christ, hurting kids of all ages can heal.

There are many secular psychological explanations and terms for why real healing occurs in a troubled youth who otherwise would have little chance of a meaningful life. We acknowledge those technical terms, but we have our own explanation. We call it a miracle. That is the business God has called us to at Ranch Hope—doing His miracles. We're eternally grateful for being His trusted ministers in living out the old adage: "Those who would expect great things from God must attempt great things for God." In keeping with our vision, we have attempted to create, in His name, not just a ranch, but a place called Hope—hope for dead-end kids.

Appendix

The Spiritual Program

The following pages embrace our philosophy of spiritual concern and commitment and can serve as a guide for anyone interested in helping troubled kids grow toward Christ. Some of the following points guide our own staff members when they first come on board.

The spiritual concern of Ranch Hope is that, in the treatment of the boys and girls entrusted to us, provision be made for recognizing, assessing, accommodating, and meeting their spiritual needs. Our prayerful petition is to see the image of God in each young person be restored to the luster of a living vital relationship with his Creator.

To many young people this will be a foreign if not hostile thought. Many despise or disdain religiosity and anticipate hypocrisy. Even day in the transactions of life, whether insignificant or momentous, they are testing and evaluating the sincerity or hypocrisy of our Christian beliefs and behavior. If, in the providence of God, a boy or girl rejects the message of salvation, he is nevertheless entitled to Christlike treatment by the agents of that message.

Spiritual care will include a comprehensive plan to provide opportunity to understand the Christian faith, which is central to treatment. This plan seeks to:

1. Emphasize that all employees are models and are therefore encouraged to grow spiritually.
2. Establish regular teaching sessions on an in-service basis to nurture this growth.

3. Follow the mandate of Scripture, "Speaking the truth in love" (Eph. 4:15) by training the staff to become more competent in both word and deed, to sensitively explain and apply Scripture to life problems.

4. Provide regular and special occasions of fellowship, study, and worship led by the ranch chaplain.

5. Understand each boy and girl as made in the image of God, yet fallen and in need of the redemptive grace of God, and therefore prayerfully integrate the treatment plan to meet this need (2 Tim. 3:16-17 and 1 Pet 1:13-25).

Each child should receive individual therapy from a trained counselor. The counselor should serve as part of a treatment that develops plans based on input from educational, social, and recreational services, childcare, chaplain, and spiritual care sources to form a comprehensive plan.

Given the emotional dysfunction of the boys and girls, it is important that spiritual emphasis should not be in conflict, nor centered on experientialism. That is, we ought to present the essentials of our evangelical faith in a manner accenting the rational elements of faith rather than the emotional.

A well-established faith can flourish in various climates. Vastly contradictory statements or approaches to presenting that faith may easily divide an already darkened mind. In summary, it is Christ and His Gospel in all its purity and simplicity, not denominationalism, that is to direct our ministering to the young people.

Ranch Hope employs a uniquely positive and comprehensive approach to residential care. Its well-rounded view of treating each young person's entire

needs—academic, physical, emotional/psychological—
also includes sensitive provision for his/her spiritual
needs.

Assisting the young people in this area offers a re-
flective avenue for helping them discover their infinite
value and worth as God's creation, defining more clearly
a personal value system consistent with our society's
Judeo-Christian perspective and drawing from a healing
inner resource often ignored.

We recognize that here is a broad diversity of religious opportunities in our culture. Our desire is to accommodate those situations where a religious
preference may or may not prevail. As a staff, our con-
victions call us to serve the boys and girls. Our creed requires us to seek nothing in return, and our beliefs allow
us to acknowledge spiritual differences.

Help for Staff

Our staff is reminded that:
1. We're working with teenagers.
2. Even "normal" teenagers are a challenge.
3. Teenagers are in between: "They aren't what they will
be, and they aren't what they used to be."
4. It is never easy to reach anyone (adult, child, or teen).
5. All will not respond.
6. We are not here to be "successful," but rather to be
"faithful." We plant, perhaps another waters, but God
gives the growth.

Because we are in a difficult work, there are certain
pitfalls we must try to avoid to help us avert even more
heartbreak:
1. We keep our spiritual life active. We take time to pray

and read the Word of God every day. "You can't give what you ain't got."

2. We don't expect too much from ourselves. We are not messiahs to troubled boys. We all have limits in any mission field. We accept our limits.

3. We keep ourselves in good shape physically.

4. We are careful of over-identification. The young people can drain us emotionally and physically. Once in a while we might find ourselves favoring one of them. We are careful not to neglect the others and spoil him/her. We know we could become too emotionally involved and become ineffective in helping them. The others would also suffer.

The Total Person

Ranch Hope is concerned for the total boy or girl. Because man has a spiritual dimension that influences his total life, we must not neglect this area in our program. In fact, it is the foundation for everything else. After years of working with troubled youth, there are certain things we have discovered.

1. There must be a structure within the religious program. It cannot be approached haphazardly with the attitude that anyone and anything will do.

2. The staff needs training in reaching the troubled boy with the Christian message. A plan and a program must be employed so that there is continuity in our approach. There must be strategy.

3. It will be necessary to deal with the boys and girls individually. Each one comes with various experiences and attitudes toward God. Through investigation, it will be possible to know each child's thinking in this regard.

A plan of testing and personal counseling will be established to know each boy or girl before we attempt to reach him/her on a spiritual level.

4. Information gained will then be passed on to staff responsible for the boy's and girl's spiritual life. Houseparents and others will be made aware of the "facts of life" that have predetermined a boy's or girl's hangups or strengths on religion.

5. Chapel, Bible class, special programs, and devotions will be geared to meet the needs of the troubled boy or girl. Variety will be the key word in communicating the gospel. Films, slides, records, magazines, and speakers will be used to help bridge any gaps.

6. It is imperative that we move cautiously toward having young people make their commitment, Why?

   a. To avoid manipulation, the boy or girl may "develop" spiritually just to get home.

   b. To avoid any attempt on his part to manipulate staff: "I'm a nice guy, growing spiritually; shouldn't I get special privileges?"

   c. To avoid having the boy pressured into spiritual growth.

7. After they do reach commitment, however, we must do all we possibly can to foster growth in them.

   a. Meet his/her needs for growth in prayer, Bible study, etc.

   b. Answer his/her inquiring mind with good literature.

   c. Get him/her involved in fellowship off the Ranch with other young people.

   d. Prepare him for the pressures from other boys and home when he attempts to show spiritual growth.

e. Begin to involve him/her in spiritual programs on the Ranch so that he/she can help
others.

f.   Communicate to his/her family that he/she
has made progress spiritually so they can be
aware of what is happening.

Our Witness

All of us have a witness to the boys and girls who
come to here. Because a houseparent or teacher is with
the child so much of the time, he or she has an even
greater witness. How can we best help them in their
spiritual life?

1. Be yourself Don't try to be the Christian you are
not. They can spot a phony.

2. Be able to quickly apologize if you goof. Everyone
knows it anyway, so take the youth aside and tell
him/her, "I'm sorry."

3. Watch your language. A slip of the tongue may
sink a boy or girl. Any curse word will be blown out of
proportion by them. It will give them an excuse to say
worse. If you do slip, quickly make amends.

4. Stay off young people's back if they aren't growing
spiritually. Don't nag or put them down for their slow
progress. You may injure your relationship.

5. Try not to harp on your own religious conversion
too often. It's nice for the boys and girls to know your
experience, but familiarity will breed contempt. "Is that
all this guy can talk about—himself?" The other danger
is that they may hold it against you when they are mad.
Your current experience of God is as important to the
boys and girls as what happened ten years ago.

6. Never treat the things of God lightly. If it is prayer before a meal, or prayer over a sick one, take your time and be serious. They will very quickly pick up on a careless attitude toward sacred things. A rushed prayer and "instant devotions" will plant seeds that will produce "weeds of the spirit."

7. Vary your devotional studies. Get some good materials so that you can cover a variety of subjects interest ing to youth. Can you imagine what it would be like to hear the same sermon in church every week? Well, they get tired of hearing John 3:16 or the story of the rich young ruler. Do some studying.

8. Spend some time talking with the young people on an informal basis. We don't have to take the boys and girls to chapel to get religion. Some "bull sessions" now and then will do as much good as herding them into the chapel. Impromptu, "off-the-cuff" discussion is great.

9. Watch your attitudes toward other religions, races, and nationalities. Prejudice is deep rooted, and we aren't here to help these roots grow deeper. Your healthy attitude toward all God's children will produce healthy youth. Don't give them anything sick.

10. Really love the Lord. Put Him first. Often, this is our best witness.

Previous Religious Life

Some of our students have already been active in Sunday School and church before coming to the ranch. Some have been baptized or confirmed in their faith. We must be careful to build upon these past positive experiences. At times, we will also want to involve local pastors, priests, or other clergypersons to help in the students' rehabilitation. As the young people progress, it is also advantageous to have them become involved in a local church.

Follow-Up

When a boy or girl makes their "decision" or "commitment" to Christ, we then become concerned for their growth. Too often in the past, our youth have made their initial step and nothing has been done in follow-up work. Remember that there will be various levels of commitment. It will be necessary to:

1. Have the boy or girl explain what has happened. Does he/she understand what it means to make a decision? Even though they may have gone forward in a church service during the "invitation to discipleship," they may be ignorant of the ramifications of this step.

2. Use what they say as a stepping stone for further counseling. Try to listen, and begin where they are. For instance, they may say, "I just feel like God wanted me to go forward," etc. This may be said in many different ways. The important thing is to try to direct the boy or girl to see that:

3. Make the following steps:

A. Accept Christ by faith.

B. Believe in Christ as personal Savior.

C. Confess those things in your life which you know were wrong before your decision.

D. Do something now to start growing. Find a way to serve.

4. Have a time of prayer with the boy or girl. Lead him/her in a prayer where he/she can say, "Lord, come into my life. I accept you as my Savior, and ask you to forgive me for the past. Help me from this time on to follow you."

5. Give the boy or girl some follow-up material and encourage him/her to attend chapel and all services where he/she can learn more, The follow-up is the most delicate and most neglected area in our ministry. The seed is planted and has started to grow, but now we must help it bear fruit.

Here are some cardinal points to remember,
1. Expect some regression. The boy or girl is not a perfected saint.
2. Expect doubts and expect to have the boy or girl question you.
3. Expect them to have pressure from others.
4. Expect the boy or girl to grow, very, very slowly at first.
5. Do not put the child down by saying, "I thought you were a Christian," if he goofs.
6. Encourage the boy or girl, and do not criticize him/her in front of others. If there is a need to reprimand him, take him aside for person-to-person counseling.

Signs of Spiritual Regression

1. Acting out in school: Refusal to do work, sleeping, showing off, disrespect to teachers, language, leaving school, lateness. Regression could begin with any one of these symptoms.

2. Acting out at home: Difficulty in getting up, late for meals, refusal to do chores or room (or a general slowdown in these areas), back talk, vulgar language, stealing from the others, running away, refusal to cooperate with daily program, misbehavior at night, failure to go to sleep.

3. Loss of interest in activities: Where they once were active, they now refuse to participate or have lost interest. In sports they will act out in the game, will not

cooperate with the other team, and will generally cause a disturbance. Does not want to go out with volunteer on staff, refuses to attend social events, stops working toward points.

4. Stops trying to advance in progress system: Where once the child may have tried to reach the next level (e.g. from ranch hand to star), now there is a lack of interest. You will hear things like:

5. Poor attitude toward the Ranch in general. You will hear comments like:

a. This is a prison. I'd rather be in reform school.

b. I don't need a place like this. I shouldn't have been sent here in the first place.

c. My buddies back home have made it. They were as bad as I am. How come I have to stay?

d. You make us stay in this hole too long.

e. This place isn't what it is publicized to be. You just put on a good show.

f. The staff is two-faced, etc.

A Good Offense: The Best Defense

Generally speaking, we cannot wait for a crisis to arise. We must stay ahead of the child's need and have a solution to a problem even before it occurs. We must all do our best to meet their spiritual needs, a true challenge in and by itself. But there is one other part: we must also meet their needs according to the position for which we were hired.

Stories From the Bible for Daily Devotions

We have listed these for staff use in aiding our boys, They are asked to record:

(a) Basic mood of the boys while they were leading in devotions.

(b) Questions they asked afterwards.

(c) Any other interesting results of using the story.

Christ's Concern for Our Needs—
Some Places to Start
(From the Book of Matthew)

1. The leper and the paralyzed boy 8:143
2. He sets us free from past sins 8:2-7
3. He fed the crowd. His help went out to all 14:14-19
4. God wants us to show help to others more than sacrifice 12:1-19
5. All nations find hope in Him 12:15-21
6. The real family of Jesus 12:46-50
7. We are somebody new, The old and new self 16:24-26
8. Start like a baby; be humble 18:1-4
9. Children come to Him (and youth, too) 19:13-15
10. God doesn't want to lose any of us 18:12-14
11. Try to help your brother who is messed up 18:15-17
12. Forgive your brother 18:21-22
13. Giving to help the poor   19:16-22
14. Give up for Jesus and get plenty back 19:27-30
15. Help for those out of work 20: 1-16
16. Service and sacrifice 20:20-34
17. Not promise, but works is best 21:28-32
18. God invites rich and poor to His feast 22:1-10
19. Get along with the guy next door 22:34-40
20. Don't be a "Holy Joe" 23:1-4,14,27,29
21. Help others get to heaven 25:31-44
22. Fighting and killing only brings more trouble 26:51-54
23. Ratting on your friends brings trouble 27:3-5
24. Jesus died for us 27:27-32,39.42,45..50 55-56
25. Victory over death 28:1,2,5,8,10

Endnotes

1 From *Frontline*, PBS, Juvenile Justice Statistics, http://ojjdp.ncjrs.org/ojstatbb/qa182.html

2 *Census of Juveniles in Residential Placement Databook*. Online. Sickmund, M., and Wan, Y. (2001).

3 *Juvenile Court Statistics 1997*, Office of Juvenile Justice and Delinquency Prevention, http:www.ncjrs.org/html/ojjdp/jcs_1007/estimdel.html#counts

4 *Census of Juveniles in Residential Placement Databook*. Online. Sickmund, M., Sladky, T.J., and Kang, Wei. (2004)

5 *General U.S. Stats* http://www.stv.net/us_stats.htm

6 *Profile '90: A Sourcebook of Juvenile Justice Data and Trends in New Jersey*. A Report of the Juvenile Delinquency Commission.

7 *Ibid*

8 Francis A. Schaeffer, *A Christian Manifesto*, Illinois: Crossway Books, 1981

9 Federal Interagency Forum on Child and Family Statistics, http://childstats.gov/ac2003/indicators.asp? IID=103&id=1

10 George Barna, "The New American Family," Moody Monthly, September 1991.

11 Linda L. Creighton, "Silent Saviors," *U.S. News & World Report*, December 16, 1991.

12 Barbara Kantrowitz, "Breaking the Divorce Cycle," *Newsweek*, January 13, 1992

13 *Washington Times*, 6/6/99.

14 http://www.marriage-relationships.com/divorce_statistics.html

15 Dr. Paul Meier, "Assessing the Damage of Divorce," *Today's Better Life*, Fall/Winter 1991.

16 *Ibid*

17 Becky Durost Fish, "Happy at Home," *Moody Monthly*, September 1991

18 Gerard Cohen-Vrignaud, The Michigan Daily 11/09/98.

19 Ken Sidey, "Stressed Out in the Suburbs," Moody Monthly, September 1991.

20 *TV Week,* The Asbury Park Press, February 6, 1992.

21 Dr. Charles R Solomon, *The Rejection Syndrome: The Need for Genuine Love and Acceptance,* Carol Stream, Illinois: Tyndale, 1982

22 Claude Lewis, "America's Worst Scandal," *Philadelphia Inquirer,* October 9, 1991

23 ABC-TV, 20/20, "Teach at Your Own Risk," February 7, 1992

24 Ike Keay, Child of Pain, Children of Joy, Grand Rapids, Michigan; Revell, 1990.

25 Bureau of Justice Statistics, U.S. Department of Justice, Office of Justice Programs http://www.ojp.usdoj.gov/bjs/prisons.htm.

26 Fox Butterfield, "U.S. Expands Its Lead in the Rate of Imprisonment," *The New York Times,* February 11, 1992.

27 *Juvenile Justice Bulletin,* Office of Juvenile Justice and Delinquency Prevention, U.S. Dept. of Justice, Washington, D.C., January 1991.

28 Dr. Charles Stanley, *The Gift of Forgiveness,* Nashville, Tennessee; Thomas Nelson Publishers, 1987.

Ranch Hope for Boys and Girls

Founded in 1964, Ranch Hope's mission is to serve "at-risk" children and families throughout the Delaware Valley. This mission is accomplished by providing:

Out-patient Counseling at our offices located in Burlington, Camden, Gloucester, and Salem counties in southern N.J.

Residential Treatment, located in Salem County, serves 56 adolescent males on a 24-hour basis for young men from 9-16 that are experiencing problems requiring temporary removal. Also at Victory House, adolescent females from 14-17 are treated in Williamstown (Gloucester County) New Jersey.

A certified Special Education school—**Strang School**—with educational and vocational services for 56 males in residential treatment as well as 20 day students from outside districts.

An affiliation with the **The Midway School** located in Lumberton, New Jersey, provides services to more than 40 students for students classified as Multiple Handicapped.

Independent Living Program, designed for males 16 and older, on the Alloway Campus in Salem County has ranch-style homes, each housing a total of three young men.

Project HOPE is a Challenge Course designed to enhance the personal goals of individuals through initiative games and high ropes programming to public school, youth groups, and adults.

Camp Edge: Day Camp experiences in sports and craft activities for 200 children of local migrant workers during the summer months.

Shelter of Hope is a temporary placement for boys and girls in cooperation with Salem County, New Jersey.

Ranch Hope has been publishing **Salt and Light in the News** for 15 years as part of its radio ministry, **Ranch Hope Radio**, which reaches the northeast part of the country. Ranch Hope Radio approaches the 50th anniversary of its daily devotional broadcast with Rev. Dave Bailey as host.

FOR ADDITIONAL INFORMATION, CONTACT:

Ranch Hope, Inc.

45 Sawmill Road, Alloway, NJ 08001

(856) 935-1555 and Fax (856) 935-5189

www.ranchhope.org

The Bailey Family

Back row: Rev. Dave and Eileen Bailey, daughter Liz and her husband Mike

Front row: Julie Bailey (Dave Jr.'s wife), grandchildren Emilee Dalessio, Gillian Bailey, Mike Dalessio, Colin Bailey, Katlyn Bailey, and Dave Bailey Jr.